FRANCIS
COPPOLA

In Cannes to promote The Rainmaker**, prior to shooting.**

FRANCIS
COPPOLA

Ronald Bergan

ORION

For Clive Hirschhorn, a friend in deed

First published in 1998 by Orion Media
An imprint of Orion Books Ltd
Orion House, 5 Upper St Martin's Lane, London WC2H 9EA

Project editor: Natasha Martyn-Johns
Designed by Leigh Jones

A CIP catalogue record for this book is available from the British Library.

ISBN 0 75281 195 9

Reproduction by Pixel Colour Ltd, London
Printed in Italy by Printers, Trento
Bound By L.E.G.O., Vicenza

Variety is a registered trademark of Reed Properties Inc.

CONTENTS

With daughter Sophia Coppola on the set of Life Without Zoe **(an episode from** New York Stories**, 1989) which they co-wrote.**

Introduction

I'm embarrassed by my duality of failure and success.
   – Francis Ford Coppola (1987)

Everything about Francis Ford Coppola is gargantuan. His successes, his failures, his girth, his appetite, his palatial homes in San Francisco, Los Angeles, New York, and in the South American republic of Belize, as well as his Napa Valley estate with its acres of vineyards.

Coppola sees himself as a benevolent godfather, embracing both his large family and familial team in his ample arms and making sure that they are well fed; gigantic pasta meals have always been an important part of both his leisure and work. 'What brings me the greatest joy is the company of nice people and to be able to go through all the rituals with them, to eat dinner with them, cook with them, talk with them. I'm very European in that respect,' he once remarked. A great deal of this Italianate generosity finds its way into most of his films, though the making of them has often been as dramatic as anything that appears on screen.

As befits someone whose films have often concerned themselves with the workings of the family, Coppola's own family occupies a central position in his life. His musician father, Carmine, composed the scores for many of his features. He and his elder brother August (father of Nicolas Cage), to whom he dedicated *Rumble Fish*, have always had a close relationship. His younger sister, the actress Talia Shire, was Connie Corleone in *The Godfather* trilogy; his second son, Roman (named after Polanski), has worked as second-unit director and production assistant on his father's movies, and daughter Sofia, who appeared in *The Outsiders* and *Rumble Fish*, had a leading role in *The Godfather Part III*.

At the age of twenty-two, his eldest son, Gian-Carlo ('Gio'), was killed in a speedboat accident. This tragedy, which occurred in 1986, cut short the young Coppola's promising film career behind the camera. Very soon after Gio's death, Coppola painfully returned to the set of *Gardens of Stone*, a picture which is concerned with the funerals of young men killed in the Vietnam War. In *The Godfather Part III*, Coppola, identifying with Michael Corleone, filmed the gunning down of Michael's daughter Mary, played by his own daughter Sofia.

Coppola's films, more than those of any other American director of his generation, lend themselves to autobiographical scrutiny. In 1973, during the making of *The Godfather Part II*, he told journalists, 'To some extent I have become Michael Corleone' because, like the mafia boss, he was 'a powerful man in charge of an entire production' and married to a non-Italian as Corleone was. While Coppola was filming *Apocalypse Now* in the jungles of the Philippines, his wife Eleanor accused him of turning into Colonel Walter Kurtz, the megalomaniac officer whom the American army wished to 'terminate with extreme prejudice'. Coppola was already considered beyond the pale by the Hollywood establishment for having set up Zoetrope, his renegade independent studio in San Francisco. *Apocalypse Now* can be read on two levels – as an essay on the evil and madness of the Vietnam War, and as a study of the director's own psychological breakdown.

It was at this period that he and his wife were going through a bad time, and almost split up. On one occasion, while Francis was arguing with Eleanor in front of the children, Sofia, their then four-year-old daughter, suddenly cried, 'Cut!' At which moment Francis came to a realization. 'Don't you think I wonder if I'm just making my next movie right now?', he yelled at Eleanor. 'Don't you think it scares me that my life is just a movie I'm making?' More than ten years later, in *Life Without Zoe* (an episode in *New York Stories*), co-written by Sofia, a twelve-year-old girl interrupts her parents' lovemaking by shouting, 'Cut!'

Of the musical *One From The Heart*, which he called a 'fantasy about romantic love, jealousy and sex', Coppola explained that he had made the film as a way of talking indirectly about a painful break-up he had just endured. In every film he makes, this director invests something of his own intellectual and emotional life. Even with *Jack*, a film about a freakish child that was no more to him than a studio chore, Coppola was able to inject memories of his own childhood when, as a polio victim, he was isolated from others.

From the outset of his career, Coppola has drawn on his personal experiences, from *You're A Big Boy Now*, about a young man's sexual education, to *The Conversation*, which expressed his own obsession with gadgetry and, most significantly, in *Tucker – The Man And His Dream*. Jeff Bridges, who played the inventor Preston Tucker, with whose independent spirit Coppola most identified, commented, 'Maybe Francis is the Tucker of our day.'

Francis Ford Coppola led the way for other 'Movie Brat' directors such as Peter Bogdanovich, George Lucas, Brian De Palma, Steven Spielberg and

Ivan the Terrible Part II **(1945), directed by Sergei Eisenstein, the great Russian director who first inspired Coppola to take up film-making.**

Martin Scorsese, who emerged from film school to storm Hollywood in the 1970s. They were exposed to classic American films at just the historical moment when these films were at last becoming intellectually respectable, convincing them that the Hollywood tradition was an honourable one. But this group also realized that the tradition was ready to be reformed and revitalized from within. There was another favourable conjunction: because the majority of people who went to the cinema in the 70s were in their teens and early twenties, the studios turned to talented film-school graduates, who could cater to the tastes of this youthful audience.

Coppola's career since has been a swashbuckling, roller-coaster affair. Not only has he always been torn between two extremes of film-making – the massive, epic form, and the small, intimate picture – but he has fluctuated between mammoth and modest hits and mammoth and modest disasters. Even his name has oscillated between the resonant trio, Francis Ford Coppola, and the more modest duo, Francis Coppola, and then back again to its full triple glory.

In a way, like Preston Tucker, the independent automobile manufacturer, Coppola was born too late to be a pioneer. His dream was to have his own studio 'run by the creative talents, free of businessmen and bureaucrats.' Ironically, Zoetrope eventually came to grief precisely because of the businessmen and bureaucrats. The paradoxes multiply throughout Coppola's life: one moment he longs to have the freedom to make small-scale low-budget movies, then plunges into monumental projects with spiralling costs; at one moment he is admiring and envious of the great non-American *auteurs*, the next he is attempting to reinstate the kind of genre movies he loved as a child – gangster pictures, *films noirs*, musicals, melodramas.

What he was really aiming for was a synthesis of the two streams of cinema. He called *You're A Big Boy Now*, 'Andy Hardy gets hit by the New Wave'; in talking about *Bram Stoker's Dracula*, he evoked the names of Georges Méliès and F. W. Murnau, and imagined *Rumble Fish* as 'an art film for kids'. Nor was he afraid to use subtitles extensively in *The Godfather* trilogy – a device unheard of in a mainstream Hollywood movie – so as to retain the authenticity of the Italian speakers.

Coppola has distributed and financed the work of Akira Kurosawa, Abel Gance and Wim Wenders, and the influence of the dynamic montage of Sergei Eisenstein, the director whose films inspired him to become a film-maker, is evident in his own montage and experiments in cinema. There are certainly elements of Eisenstein's baroque *Ivan the Terrible* in *The Godfather* trilogy, and the prologue to *Bram Stoker's Dracula* owes much to the operatic extravagances of *Alexander Nevsky*.

Perhaps the best illustration of this synthesis is *The Conversation*. Fundamentally a detective story with a classic narrative structure and all the conventions of the genre – investigation, threat, revelation – it is invaded by devices taken from art cinema. According to critics David Bordwell and Janet Staiger, '*The Conversation* exemplifies how the New Hollywood has absorbed narrational strategies of the art cinema while controlling them within a coherent genre framework.' What is fascinating about Coppola's films is how close to the borders of this framework he risks going, and the games of brinkmanship he plays with casts, film crews, audiences and investors alike.

1   A Boy Called 'Science'

The popular kid is out having a good time. He doesn't sit around thinking about who he is or how he feels. But the kid who is ugly, sick, miserable or schlumpy sits around heartbroken and thinks. He's like an oyster growing a pearl of feelings which becomes the basis of an art.

Someone once said, 'Never trust anyone with three names.' Knowing this expression, Francis Ford Coppola decided to drop the middle name from the credits of his films in 1977. However, that middle name has appeared, disappeared and reappeared throughout his career. There has been much dispute as to where the Ford came from. Some believe that his prescient parents named him after the great film director John Ford, but Francis Coppola was, in fact (albeit indirectly) named after Henry Ford, the automobile manufacturer. This is ironic in that one of Coppola's idols was Preston Tucker, the free-spirited car designer, who was put out of business by big companies like Ford. The parallel between Coppola and Tucker, the hero of the director's 1988 biopic, *Tucker: The Man and his Dream*, are more than coincidental.

Francis Ford Coppola was born on 7 April 1939 in the Henry Ford Hospital in Detroit, Michigan, where his musician father, Carmine, was official arranger for the *Ford Sunday Evening Hour* on CBS radio, a programme of 'good music'. Hence the middle name. Over the years, however, various commentators have thought his middle name should have been 'extravagance' or 'megalomania'.

Both sets of Francis' grandparents had emigrated from Southern Italy to the USA around the turn of the century. His parental grandfather was Augustino Coppola, who came from peasant stock in Apulia, on the Gulf of Taranto. Augustino's wife, Maria Zaza, though pure Italian, had been brought up in Tunis and spoke French and Arabic as well as Italian. They had seven sons, all of whom showed some musical talent, especially Carmine, who earned a scholarship to New York's prestigious Julliard School from where he graduated in 1928, and Anton, his uncle, who became a conductor. Coppola declared that the scene in *The Godfather Part II* where the gunsmith has the little boy play the flute, was based on his grandfather and father. The importance of his family and his Italian background were certainly an incalculable advantage to him when tackling *The Godfather* trilogy.

Through a fellow student at the Julliard, Carmine met, fell in love with and married Italia Pennino. Italia's father, Francesco Pennino, a songwriter and lyricist, had come to America as Enrico Caruso's pianist. In the USA, Francesco ran a movie theatre in Brooklyn, showing mostly Italian silent pictures.

In 1934 Carmine and Italia had their first child, August Floyd Coppola. Francis arrived five years later when Carmine was first flautist with the Detroit Symphony Orchestra and official arranger for the *Ford Sunday Evening Hour* on CBS. Soon afterwards the family moved back to New York, where Carmine had been appointed first flautist under Toscanini in the NBC Symphony Orchestra. 'My father would take me at 5 p.m. to studio 8H at NBC and put me in a glass box so I could watch Toscanini, and there'd be a knob in there that controlled the volume, and that just blew me away when I was a kid, when I realized that picture and sound were not connected!' During the same period, Francis' uncle, Anton Coppola, was conductor of the orchestra at the Radio City Music Hall. (In 1992, Coppola hired Anton to conduct the orchestra on the soundtrack of *Bram Stoker's Dracula*.)

Francis remembered being taken backstage at the Radio City Music Hall every month as a child. 'We could see the chorus girls and the Rockettes, and watch my uncle conduct. There was a tremendous musical/theatre/opera influence on us.' Although his three musicals (*Finian's Rainbow*, *One From The Heart* and *The Cotton Club*) were among his least successful pictures, the musical element and rhythmic cutting in Coppola's films is of prime significance. However, despite this environment, Carmine had different plans for his two sons. August was told he would grow up to be a doctor and Francis would become an engineer. There were no plans yet for Talia, the boys' baby sister, who was born in 1946. She would, of course, become the actress Talia Shire, best known for her role as Sylvester Stallone's long-suffering wife in the *Rocky* movies, and her appearances as Connie Corleone in *The Godfather* saga.

Francis, who attended New York City School PS 109, the same school attended by the young hero of *You're A Big Boy Now*, was not a particularly gifted pupil. Then something happened that changed the course of Francis' entire life. One summer when he was ten years old, he went on a Cub Scout trip.

It rained tremendously, and our tents all got soaked, and we were sleeping in the water [Coppola recalled]. At home, I got up and had a stiff neck. So I went to my father, who told me to go to school. But it kept bothering me, so I went to the school nurse. Before I knew it I was being whisked away in an ambu-lance. My mother was crying . . . . The first night was pretty painful, and I kept calling out for my mother, but I was more frightened by the cries of the other kids. Next day, I was in a bed in some other part of the hospital. I remember I tried to get out of the bed, and when I got out I went down; I couldn't lift myself up. That's how I discovered that I had lost the use of my left arm.

Francis had been struck down with polio. He returned home in a few weeks, his left leg, left arm, left side and entire back paralysed. Polio is a heavily contagious disease. The boy had to spend months confined to his bedroom with no other children for company, other than an occasional glimpse of his brother and sister. This experience was alluded to in *The Conversation*, when Harry Caul (Gene Hackman) talks about being paralysed for months during childhood. Coppola recalled it again over four decades later when he was making *Jack*, which tells the story of a ten-year-old boy with a condition that ages him four years for every one. 'I remember being pinned to this bed, and longing for friends and company,' Coppola explained. 'When I read *Jack* I was moved because that was precisely his problem; there are no children in his life.'

To occupy the weary hours, Francis would watch as much TV as there was in a day. One of his favourite shows was *Horn and Hardart's Children's Hour* each Sunday morning. It was from watching this programme that the idea of his own Zoetrope studio had its genesis, a studio 'where we could work together like children, with music, puppets, scenery, lights, dramatic action, whatever we wanted to do.'

He also had a tape recorder and a 16mm projector. 'One of my problems was figuring out how to synchronize the sound between the projector and the tape in the recorder. I'd invent all the "soundtrack" myself, imitating Mickey Mouse and so on, and then I'd start the machines in sync. But I could never quite get it.' It was the beginning of his abiding interest in the technology behind the making of his films.

Although Francis was told he would never walk again, and was warned that he could damage his muscles if he crawled around, Carmine brought a physiotherapist to the house. He gradually got Francis to lift his arm and slowly got him walking again. Thus, after nine months of being restricted to the house, Francis returned to school. He was left with a limp, something he shared with the great French director Jean Renoir, one of his teachers at UCLA. It was not a pronounced limp, but, as Coppola was aware, 'you can always tell when you put your arm around a girl and you walk with her – that's when it's magnified!'

Rumble Fish, which centres on the strong bond between The Motorcycle Boy (Mickey Rourke) and his hero-worshipping younger brother Rusty-

James (Matt Dillon), was dedicated to 'my older brother August Coppola, my first and best teacher'. Five years his senior, 'Augie', as he was called, was tall, dark and handsome, and had no trouble in finding girls, whereas 'I was funny-looking, not good at school, and didn't know any girls . . . . Augie was the smart one and Talia was the pretty one.'

Apart from *Rumble Fish*, the relationship between brothers also features strongly in *The Godfather* trilogy and *The Cotton Club*, in which there are two sets. Augie would take Francis with him to movie matinees at the Center Theater on Queens Boulevard, around 45th Street. As Francis remarked, 'A lot of brothers would dump a kid five years younger, but he would always take me everywhere.' Among Francis' favourite films were three fantasy pictures based on H.G. Wells: *Things to Come*, *The War of the Worlds* and *The Man Who Could Work Miracles*, as well as Alexander Korda's *The Thief of Bagdad*, and Bela Lugosi in *Dracula* (very different from his own version some decades later). Evidently, he was always excited by the 'magical' element in movies.

At the same time, Francis was obsessed by the technology and gadgets of all sorts, so much so that other kids gave him the nickname of 'Science'. Describing Harry Caul in *The Conversation*, Coppola noted, 'Somewhere along the way he must have been one of those kids who's sort of a weirdo in high school. You know, the kind of technical freak who's president of the radio club. When I was a kid I was one of those guys like I was just describing.'

Francis decided he wanted to be a nuclear scientist when he grew up, and managed to save fifty dollars to buy a toy atomic energy lab, with a Geiger counter and a cloud chamber with a radioactive needle. He was also fascinated by secret microphones, another passion that resurfaced in *The Conversation*, though the technology of bugging was far less sophisticated when he was a child. 'When I was a kid about thirteen or fourteen, there was a tremendous sense of power in putting microphones around to hear other people', Coppola remembered. 'I even had a plan to put microphones in the radiators of all the rooms in the house so that I could tune in on what I was going to get for Christmas.' In addition, he would edit pieces of film shot by his family, attempt to build a television, and he knew how to make all kinds of explosives.

In the meantime, the now fifteen-year-old Francis had taken up the tuba, and was enrolled at the New York Military Academy at Cornwall-on-Hudson, which had given him a scholarship on the strength of his playing. He disliked the place and its emphasis on sports, as well as hating the way 'the older cadets were always brutalizing the younger cadets,' something he played down in *Gardens of Stone*, his film set in a military academy. After eighteen months at the Academy, Francis ran away, making his way to Manhattan, where he wandered around the city

Watching rushes from Rumble Fish **(1983), which Coppola dedicated to his older brother August. Matt Dillon, hand on head, is behind the director.**

for some days. Some of his experiences on the run are evoked in *You're A Big Boy Now*, especially the long sequence when Bernard Chanticleer wanders around the sex shops of 42nd Street. When Francis returned to high school, he continued to play the tuba in the military band, but theatre and the movies were his real loves.

Carmine was doing reasonably well and the family moved to Great Neck, Long Island to a pleasant house with a yard. There Francis tried to make friends with the 'beautiful' children of the Long Island families, but was rejected by them. Therefore, he hung out with the 'rocks', the ducktailed sons of those who worked for the wealthy families. They formed themselves into a gang called the Bay Rats, echoing the rival youth gangs in *The Outsiders* – the 'Socs' (the rich kids) and the 'Greasers' (the working-class kids) – where Coppola's sympathies are plainly with the latter group.

On the strength of plays he had written, Francis won a drama scholarship to Hofstra University at Hempstead, Long Island where August had studied. In the excellent Theater Department, Francis staged a one-act play by Eugene O'Neill called *The Rope*, and a musical called *Inertia*, which was based on *The Man Who Could Work Miracles*, for which future singer Steve Lawrence composed the music. For a production of *A Streetcar Named Desire* he cast Bob Spiotta as Stanley Kowalski. Spiotta, a husky football player, would later become head of Zoetrope Studios in Los Angeles, and Ronald Colby, who appeared in *Finian's Rainbow*, had the lead in *Picnic*. Among other schoolmates was James Caan (*The Rain People*, *The Godfather*, *Gardens of Stone*). At Hofstra, Francis was 'top guy', although he had a reputation as an uncouth loudmouth. His description of Preston Tucker could almost have been about himself. 'He talked too much and had too big a mouth. When you tell people your dreams out of enthusiasm, somehow it makes them seem disgruntled.'

Francis graduated from Hofstra in 1959 with a BA in Theatre Arts. With money he gained from selling his car, he bought a 16mm movie camera, having already made a few 8mm shorts, but he had no intention of becoming a film director. However, one day at the Museum of Modern Art cinema, he saw Sergei Eisenstein's *October*, known in America as *Ten Days That Shook The World*. The impact on him of the silent 1928 film, the apotheosis of Eisenstein's 'montage of film attractions', depicting the triumph of the Russian Revolution, was immeasurable. 'On Monday I was in the theater, and on Tuesday I wanted to be a film-maker,' Coppola later asserted.

2 Peeping Francis

I had so little money that I had no place to sleep except on our sets. It was rather depressing to shoot these wild bedroom scenes and then have to sleep in the same bed at night.

In the autumn of 1960, Coppola entered the University of California at Los Angeles Film School to get a master's degree. Among his teachers was Dorothy Arzner who had been a leading editor and director in the 1930s. She encouraged Francis to make his first film at UCLA, a short psychological horror movie. Obviously inspired by Edgar Allan Poe's *William Wilson*, and called *The Two Christophers*, it was about a boy who finds that another boy has the same name as his and decides to kill the usurper. This was followed by *Ayamonn the Terrible*, the title of which was a pun on Eisenstein's *Ivan the Terrible*. It contained a reference to the opening scene of *October*, when the head of the statue of the Tsar is dismantled, and later restored in a reverse shot.

Coppola's story was about an Irish sculptor called Ayamonn Moureen who works non-stop for four days and nights sculpting a twelve-foot head of himself. On its completion, he has a nightmare in which the head begins to shout at him. In the dream he chops off the statue's mouth, but when Ayamonn wakes up, he finds he has been struck dumb. Freudians might be tempted to analyse it as Coppola's own nightmare, seeing his inflated ego as an obstacle to his own creative abilities.

The film was photographed in eight days, partly by Steve Burum, who was later to shoot *The Outsiders* and *Rumble Fish*. For the image in the dream sequence when the head yells at the sculptor, Coppola ran the camera backwards, getting people to throw leaves and earth at the statue so that it looked as though it were spewing it all out.

Although Coppola was constantly broke during his first year at UCLA – he could hardly exist on the ten dollars a week his father sent him – he managed to raise three thousand dollars to make a short nudie movie. He was inspired to make *The Peeper*, because he felt he could do better than Russ Meyer's first 'skin flick', *The Immortal Mr Teas*, which had made a lot of money in the suburban art theatres the previous year. Coppola's own sex romp was about a voyeuristic little man who goes to extraordinary lengths to spy on a redheaded woman during her sessions at an 'artistic' photographic studio. He first puts his eye to a peephole in a door but is scared away by a plain secretary. He then buys a telescope but only sees the model's belly-button. By means of a series of pulleys and ropes, he pulls himself up the side of a building and peeps through the window with binoculars before he takes a tumble. He climbs on the roof and looks through the skylight, and digs a tunnel to come up in the studio. It might be possible to see in this peeping tommyrot a dry run for *The Conversation*, about another kind of eavesdropping.

Coppola explained how the medium-length *The Peeper* was developed into the first feature film credited to him:

> Some people saw it and offered to buy, but they themselves had shot a vast amount of footage of a Western nudie, about a drunken cowboy who hits his head and sees naked girls instead of cows. They wanted me to intercut my film with theirs . . . . So they gave me money and we devised a plot gimmick whereby both characters meet and tell their stories . . . under the title *Tonight for Sure*. Sixty to seventy per cent was not my work, but I was so eager for recognition that I shot the credit sequence and printed 'Directed by Francis Ford Coppola' on the screen!

The gimmick was to have a cowboy arrive on Sunset Strip where he meets the little man (from *The Peeper*), who is running a campaign against the 'evils of feminine exposure'. They go to a strip club where they tell each other the stories of how they came to take up the crusade, continually drinking and moving closer to the stage. The crude 'nudie' jumps from the Western, the Peeping Tom tale, and the linking scenes in the club, where girls are stripping. The colour photography is muddy, the humour heavy (we quickly get the point that the two men are lubricious hypocrites), the script leaden, but the film's *raison d'être*, to display a range of naked girls in many different situations, is modestly achieved. There is no full frontal nudity, and the professional strippers perform in the best possible taste, each one with a gimmick, like the three wise-cracking strippers in the Broadway musical *Gypsy*.

His next 'nudie cutie' was called *The Playgirls and the Bellboy*. Taking a long German melodrama, that included one sequence with a group of nude dancers, Coppola added about forty minutes of nude sequences in colour and 3-D. These softest of soft-core movies brought Coppola enough money to buy an Italian motorscooter, and give him a taste for commercial film-making.

Although among his earliest films, and plainly made for money alone, these 'skin flicks' do reflect a certain attitude to women that exists

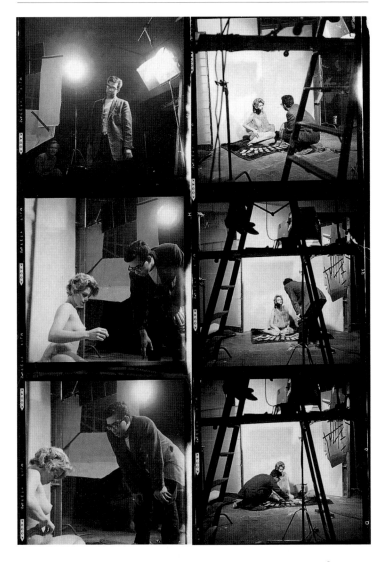

The twenty-two-year-old UCLA student directing scenes from
The Peeper, **which would be expanded to become** Tonight
For Sure **(1962).**

throughout much of Coppola's work. As a whole, women play only conventional or peripheral roles in his male-dominated world. Apart from *The Rain People* and *Peggy Sue Got Married*, the only two of his films to date with women in the leads, they do not feature significantly. In *The Godfather* trilogy, women are only there to support the men as wives and daughters; there was little room for them in either *The Outsiders* or *Rumble Fish*, films about male bonding. The only women in *Apocalypse Now* are the Playboy Bunnies dancing for the mammoth audience of horny soldiers.

Just as Coppola was about to embark on a career as a director, he was called up for military duty, although he still had a slight limp from the polio he had had as a child. He was also classified as a minor epileptic. Determined to flunk the physical, Coppola stayed up the entire night before, drinking endless mugs of hot coffee, while writing seventy to eighty pages of a screenplay called *Pilma, Pilma*. Despite this, he passed the physical the next morning, only fainting eight hours later. However, an appeal on medical grounds was upheld, and he eventually managed to avoid the draft. Subsequently, *Pilma, Pilma* would win him the Samuel Goldwyn Prize.

While still at UCLA, Coppola had a most propitious meeting. Independent producer Roger Corman, the inventor of the 'Z-movie', had bought the rights to a Soviet cold-war science fiction film (*Nebo Zowet*), about Russian astronauts triumphing over cowardly American ones. 'I needed someone to edit and dub it, so I contacted the Film Department of UCLA and asked them to send some students along,' recalled Corman. 'I talked with several and chose Francis. He was the first of the group that would become famous. He shot a couple of special effects scenes for *Battle Beyond the Sun*.' Coppola actually wrote some new dialogue – the cold-war politics disappeared – and shot a battle scene with monsters, including a penis monster against a vagina monster!

Coppola, who was credited as associate producer, worked on the film for a few months for a fee of two hundred and fifty dollars. Though still a post-graduate student at UCLA, he soon became Corman's right-hand man, serving as script doctor, production assistant, dialogue director, second-unit director and sound recordist, all for four hundred dollars a week. In these various capacities, he worked on horror quickies such as *The Tower of London* and *The Premature Burial*.

In 1962, Corman shipped his small unit to Ireland for *The Young Racers*, a youth-oriented movie which was mostly filmed in five days on location. It told of a reckless racing driver (William Campbell) with the Lotus team. According to Campbell, Coppola, who shot most of the racing footage as second-unit director, was foolhardy. 'He picks up the goddam hand-held camera, he gets out on the racetrack, and he's shooting pictures of these damn racing drivers driving past him within six feet!'

When Corman was about to return to the USA for *The Raven*, another of his successful Edgar Allan Poe movies, Coppola pitched an idea for a film to his mentor. *Psycho* was a big hit at the time, so he thought about a low-budget horror film 'with a lot of people getting killed with axes and so forth'. Francis described the opening scene to Corman thus: 'A man goes to a pond and takes off his clothes, picks up five dolls, ties them together, goes under the water, dives down, where he finds the body of a seven-year-old girl with her hair floating in the current. The man rushes to the surface and yells, "Axed to death!".' Corman said, 'Change the man to a woman and you've got a picture, kid!' Such was the genesis of Coppola's first real feature film.

3 Bloody Business

We were young and making a feature film. I think that kind of enthusiasm has a lot to do with the fact that when you're young your standards are low. If you shoot something that looks like a real movie, that puts you into euphoria.

Dementia was a title Roger Corman wanted to use for a film, but had no story, so he attached it to Coppola's first feature. Because there was another film of the same name (directed by John Parker in 1955) it became *Dementia 13*. Corman agreed to put up an initial twenty thousand dollars towards the cost, and to inject a few thousand more towards the end of the shooting. Raymond Stross, an English producer at Dublin's Ardmore Studios, gave Coppola a further twenty thousand in exchange for British distribution rights.

Coppola left for Ireland in the summer of 1962 with a few colleagues and no script. The crew of nine included Coppola's sixteen-year-old sister Talia, and the cast consisted of actors who had been in *The Young Racers*. William Campbell played the lead, joined by Patrick Magee, Luana Anders and several members of the Abbey Theatre. They all worked for one per cent of the profits. John Vicario, who was to assist on the cinematography, asked if his girlfriend Eleanor Neil could accompany him to Ireland at her own expense. The twenty-six-year-old Eleanor, a shy, soft-spoken ash-blonde, who had graduated from the UCLA Art Department, was studying for a master's degree and teaching design classes. She assisted the art director, and got a screen credit as set director. During the shooting, she and Francis became attracted to each other, and by the end, they were in love.

Dementia 13 was shot in two weeks on location in two rambling rural manor houses in Bray, and a further ten days at Ardmore Studios in Dublin. Coppola sent the dailies to Corman in California, who kept cabling him to add 'more sex and violence.' Despite these instructions, the only love scene is a tame roll in the hay. After the day's work, Coppola would spend most nights typing the next day's script on mimeograph masters,

The young and relatively slim Coppola poses while filming the 'nudie' picture, Tonight For Sure **(1962).**

which his production staff would copy in the morning. Hectic as it was, Coppola has said that *Dementia 13* was the only film he really enjoyed the process of shooting. Despite the telegrams from Corman, Francis felt he was in control, surrounded by professional people for the first time.

At the end of the shoot, he and Eleanor went to Dubrovnik in Yugoslavia where he spent eight weeks working as script supervisor and editor on a whodunnit called *Operation Titian* in which Corman had invested. When Corman received the picture it was unreleasable. Footage was therefore cannibalised from several Corman pictures, including *Blood Bath* and *Track of the Vampire*.

When Coppola returned from Europe to Los Angeles, he found that *Pilma Pilma*, the quickie script he had written on the night before his army physical, had won the Samuel Goldwyn Prize – two thousand dollars. He then sold it for five thousand dollars, but it was never filmed. 'All that money for one passionate night of writing,' Coppola remarked. But his joy was short-lived. When Corman saw *Dementia 13*, he found the plot virtually incomprehensible. He was so furious that he broke a pencil over his knee and stormed out of the screening room. Francis followed him out and there was a vociferous argument, during which Coppola managed to convince Corman that all it needed was additional linkage material to clear up the plot. Coppola then wrote several new sequences, including a new opening, and shot extra scenes on the lake in Griffith Park and underwater scenes in an LA swimming pool.

But producer and director continued to have disagreements about the editing. Corman wanted the dialogue dubbed, and a voice-over narration for the scenes he found confusing. He also felt the film needed more violence to make it commercially viable. When Francis resisted, Corman got Jack Hill (the cinematographer on *Tonight For Sure*) to write further scenes without Coppola's involvement. 'Roger wanted some more violence, another axe murder at least – which he got, though not from me,' he explained.

Coppola felt Corman had betrayed him. Nevertheless when he was asked to go up to Big Sur to shoot some footage on *The Terror*, starring Jack Nicholson, he went. The sets for *The Raven* were still in place, and Boris Karloff was still under contract, so hastily written scenes were handed to a number of people, including Monte Hellman, Jack Hill, Nicholson himself and Coppola. Francis shot an enormous amount of film, which made him unpopular with Corman. When he returned to LA, he told Corman he was quitting *The Terror*. A week later, on 2 February 1963, he and Eleanor were married in Las Vegas. (Francis later renewed his friendship with Roger Corman, who has a cameo in *The Godfather Part II*.)

Most of *Dementia 13* takes place at Castle Haloran, where Lady Haloran (Eithne Dunn) is still mourning the death of her little daughter, who drowned in the pond seven years before. Her scheming daughter-in-law, Louise (Luana Anders), for some obscure reason, steals some toys from the child's nursery, strips down to her underwear (surprisingly, the only erotic moment), dives underwater and ties the toys to branches at the bottom so they will soon float to the surface. As she is about to get out of the pond, an unseen man takes an axe to her. The same killer later chops off the head (obviously and risibly a wax model) of a poacher (played by Karl Schanzer, the Peeping Tom from *Tonight For Sure*). Suspicion falls on taciturn sculptor Richard Haloran (William Campbell), but it is, not unexpectedly, his younger brother Billy (Bart Patton) who is exposed at the end by a trap set by the family doctor (sinister Patrick Magee).

With its murky plot, suspect psychology and rather stilted dialogue and acting, *Dementia 13* bears all the marks of a horror quickie, and many of the clichés of the genre: an owl hooting in close-up, an old dark castle, a secret, locked room, creaking footsteps down a corridor . . . . But, although it is likely to provoke more giggles than gasps, it is quite an effective and atmospheric little shocker, well photographed in black and white by Charles Hanawalt. The influence of *Psycho* is blatant, mainly in that the blonde heroine is killed half-way into the film, and that the killer is a disturbed young man. There are also elements of Roger Corman's Poe movies, but there are some personal touches despite the financial and artistic restrictions imposed on its young director.

The pre-credit sequence between Louise and her husband in the middle of a lake in a rowing boat, in which he dies of a heart attack, is accompanied by the tinny, distorted sound of rock music coming from his cassette player, adding a spiky tension. Louise throws the dead man overboard, an incident which foreshadows her own later demise. In the child's nursery there is a clockwork monkey wielding an axe, and a nursery rhyme ('Little fishy in the brook, poppa's hanged you on a hook . . .') serves as a clue to the murderer, all of which relates to Billy's childhood trauma. There is also the theme of familial violence and a complicated fraternal relationship, later greatly developed and deepened by Coppola in subsequent movies.

When *Dementia 13* opened in September 1963, some cinemas instigated a gimmick in which audiences had to take a D-13 shock test before they were allowed in. The film, which got mixed reviews, did make a little money at the box-office.

After Coppola had completed *Dementia 13*, he received a call from Seven Arts who offered him three hundred and seventy-five dollars a week to write the screenplay for *Reflections in a Golden Eye*, based on the Carson

McCullers novel. George Byron Sage, one of the studio's readers, wrote of the result: 'Morally this screenplay is shocking and revolting, dramatically it is completely absorbing and utterly fascinating . . . it is the most brilliant dramatization of this very challenging novel that we are likely to see. If he is a new writer for the screen . . . his talent is something the entire industry will recognize.'

John Huston, who was scheduled to direct the film, liked Coppola's screenplay, but he wasn't yet ready to start work. When he made the film, in 1967, he used another script. However, Seven Arts upped Coppola's salary to five hundred dollars a week on a three-year contract, so that when he left UCLA at the end of 1963, he, Ellie and newly-born Gian-Carlo were able to move to a big house in Mandeville Canyon. After having lived frugally at Laurel Canyon this was luxury, but Francis continued to save money to be able to make a movie of his own. When he had accumulated twenty thousand dollars, he risked it all on the stock market and lost it, so was forced to continue writing screenplays, one of which was *This Property Is Condemned*, an adaptation from a Tennessee Williams one-act play. It was to star Elizabeth Taylor, who wanted Montgomery Clift as her leading man and her husband Richard Burton to direct. When the studio refused, she quit. Fourteen other writers came in, although Coppola finally got a co-screenwriting credit on the finished 1966 film starring Natalie Wood and Robert Redford, and directed by Sydney Pollack.

In the spring of 1966, Francis, a pregnant Ellie, and Gian-Carlo went to Paris, where he was one of ten writers (including Gore Vidal) on the sprawling all-star *Is Paris Burning?* about the liberation of Paris from the Germans in World War II. The French director René Clément had no control over the script and had to give way to the producer, something Francis found hard to take. 'I quit and was fired at the same time,' he said. However, during the stay in Paris, his second son Roman (named after Roman Polanski) was born, and he wrote a screenplay for himself to direct. The screenplay, aptly titled *You're A Big Boy Now*, would see him emerge as a fully-fledged director for the first time.

4 Rites of Passage

You're a Big Boy Now is a very flashy film in many ways. I would like to be more subtle. But flashy films do attract attention, and whether it is good or bad, my picture succeeded on that score.

Coppola had read and liked a sentimental-education novel by the British author David Benedictus entitled *You're A Big Boy Now*, which related the adventures of a melancholy young clerk in a London shoe shop. Francis bought an option for a thousand dollars, and transposed the story to New York, the shoe shop becoming the New York Public Library. He approached Roger Corman with it, but Seven Arts insisted that, because he had written the script while in their employment (i.e. during the making of *Is Paris Burning?*), it belonged to them. Coppola agreed, but insisted on directing the film. Seven Arts offered him a fee of eight thousand dollars for writing and directing, plus ten per cent of the profits. With a budget in the region of $800,000, *You're A Big Boy Now* would be shot mostly on location in Manhattan, for which Coppola obtained permission from Mayor John Lindsay to film a number of sequences in the New York Public Library.

At the start, Coppola rehearsed with the actors for a week, allowing them a great deal of improvisation, and then brought in an audience to see how they would react to the lines. When it came to the first day of shooting, twenty-seven-year-old Coppola, faced with forty crew members, found that he was so nervous he had no idea how to begin. He therefore dismissed everyone so he could have an hour to think things through. When he returned and got his first shot out of the way, everything started to flow.

Taking his cue from the French New Wave directors, Coppola shot a lot of the film with a hand-held Arriflex in order to follow his young hero Bernard Chanticleer (played by Canadian Peter Kastner) through the New York streets uninhibited. He also shot at night, without camera lights, using Eastman's new high speed 5251 colour film, which allowed him and his cinematographer Andy Laszlo to ride around in a convert-

ible, pointing his camera at anything he wanted. The location shooting
all over the city is one of the major strengths of the film: the camera
tracks Bernard as he walks around the grind houses and porn shops of
42nd Street; as he chases a kite through Central Park, and as he himself
is chased through a department store. The latter sequence was shot in
Macy's department store at 11 a.m. with the customers unaware that a
film was being made. 'It was terrific,' Coppola recalled. 'It started a riot.
Little old ladies were having heart attacks. One guy grabbed Peter
[Kastner] and started a fight with him – which Peter won. Some kids
started ripping Peter's clothes off of him. My only regret is that we didn't
have thirty cameras to get everything down on film.' A little later, in an
article in the *New York Times*, Coppola was called 'the Orson Welles of
the hand-held camera.'

The film took twenty-nine days to shoot, a short schedule for
Hollywood but long by the Corman standards Francis was used to. Before
the premiere, Coppola completed his most important screenplay to that
date. It was a study of the tyrannical and controversial General George
S. Patton, which Francis had been given six months to complete. The
reason the producer at 20th Century-Fox, Frank McCarthy, hired
Coppola, was his mistaken belief that he had come from a military background. 'What they didn't know was that my only military background
was playing tuba in a military academy band.' Francis explained. 'It's
ridiculous. I was only five when World War II ended. But since *Is Paris
Burning?* I've become a Second World War specialist.' But with fifty
thousand dollars offered for the script, he took on the task, reading as
much as he could about Patton in a short time. At the end of 1965 there
was no director set, and it only reached the screen four years later at a
time when it helped him out of one of the several deep holes in his career.

In March 1967, *You're A Big Boy Now* opened in New York to reasonable
reviews, and was well-received at the Cannes Film Festival in May that
year. The film has a delightful, youthful free-wheeling quality that
reflects the life of nineteen-year-old Bernard Chanticleer who works in
the cellars of the New York Public Library, moving around the book
shelves on roller skates. Both his overbearing philandering father (thirty-
six-year-old Rip Torn, with grey streaks in his hair), the director of
the library, and his possessive mother (Geraldine Page), treat him like
a child. When he finally escapes from their Long Island home and
gets an apartment in Greenwich Village, he meets the girl of his
dreams, an Off-Broadway actress named Barbara Darling (Elizabeth
Hartman). After she deceives him with his more experienced work mate
(Tony Bill), he goes back to the sweet girl who loves him (Karen Black,
in her film debut).

You're A Big Boy Now is very much a movie of the mid-1960s, directed by someone who had absorbed the innovations of both the French and the British New Wave – jump cuts, improvisation, deconstructed narratives, and quotes from literature and other films. A young man's film about a young man, it is full of clever visual tricks and a few in-jokes: scenes from *Dementia 13* are being shown on the wall of a disco, and in a mini flashback Barbara is seen as a schoolgirl watching Roger Corman's *The Pit and the Pendulum*. Peter Kastner has just the right kind of naive charm to carry the film, while Elizabeth Hartman, having blossomed from her previous mousy roles in *A Patch of Blue* and *The Group*, makes a perfect sexual tease from the moment a long tracking shot picks her up sensationally entering the reading room of the library in the pre-credit sequence. Her entrance, and various other scenes, owe more than a little to John Schlesinger's *Billy Liar* (1963), also about a day-dreaming nerd.

'I wanted it to be a farce,' Coppola explained. 'Because I think growing up when you are nineteen is very serious, but when you are twenty-eight it's a farce. So I wanted to have the craziness of that kind of world.' Unfortunately, the farcical elements get out of hand in the last quarter, and the older characters – the parents, a cop called Francis and, particularly, the boy's prim landlady Miss Thing (Julie Harris), develop into exaggerated caricatures, and the comedy becomes broader and sillier. Yet it is no more so than many a 1960s farce, such as *What's New Pussycat?* (1965), and the numbers, by John Sebastian, including the title song, performed by The Lovin' Spoonful, give the film a musical lift. 'I wanted to make a film that had the energy of a musical comedy,' commented Coppola. 'I always thought of *You're A Big Boy Now* as a musical film.' He would soon have the chance to direct a fully-fledged Hollywood musical.

5 Shall We Dance?

> I was brought in to direct a project that had already been cast and structured. I was also working in a big studio, in a methodology I didn't understand very well. I'd express some doubts about the way things were going, and the people around me would say, 'It's going great!' We had no sour notes on *Finian's Rainbow*. Everyone kept saying how terrific everything was all the time. They were sincere, their motives were pure.

While completing *You're A Big Boy Now*, Coppola declared, 'My idea of making a movie is to take four guys and you go out and grab a movie. But there's so much money involved here that I go around all day depressed . . . . With all these big stars and all these producers with dollar signs in their eyes, I don't know what I'm doing anymore.' But, especially in the movie industry, the best laid plans . . . . Early in 1967, Coppola got a call from Warners offering him the musical *Finian's Rainbow*. As Francis had always loved musicals – his father had spent much of his life either conducting or orchestrating musical comedies – the idea of directing a large-scale film musical greatly appealed to him, especially as Fred Astaire had been cast in the lead.

The 1947 E. Y. Harburg-Burton Lane hit Broadway musical was a parable set in Rainbow Valley, Missitucky. Finian McLonergan (Fred Astaire) and his daughter Sharon (Petula Clark) arrive in Rainbow Valley, Missitucky from Ireland, having fled Og, the leprechaun (Tommy Steele) from whom Finian has stolen a crock of gold. Og follows Finian to Missitucky, where he turns a bigoted sheriff (Keenan Wynn) into a black man, who learns the evils of racism. All ends happily when Og falls in love and becomes a human, and Finian goes on his merry way. The moral is that gold is a base metal and it is people who constitute the world's wealth.

Although its book was a rather dated blend of blarney and social satire, the show did contain some grand tunes such as 'How Are Things in Glocca Morra?', 'That Old Devil Moon' and 'If This Isn't Love'. Coppola saw it as an opportunity to give Carmine the job of doing the

Directing Fred Astaire in Finian's Rainbow **(1968).**

orchestrations, and to create some vibrant open-air dance numbers, for which he would have the services of the celebrated choreographer Hermes Pan (who was signed to the film at Astaire's insistence).

It sounded too good to be true. It was. Unfortunately, Warners' projected budget was $3.5 million, considerably less than that of any other musical being made at the time. Coppola wanted to shoot in Kentucky, but the studio refused because they wanted to use some of the expensive sets left over from the recently completed *Camelot*. Thus, most of the film was made on the Warners back lot, with Coppola making good use of only eight days of location work in Monterey, Carmel, and San Francisco.

After five weeks' rehearsal, the seven-week shoot began on 26 June 1967. Midway through, Hermes Pan was fired after Coppola claimed his dances were 'abysmal'. Pan, who retained his credit on the film, later described Coppola as 'a real pain. He knew very little about dancing and musicals . . . . These schoolboys who studied at UCLA think they're geniuses, but there is a lot they don't understand.' Ignoring Astaire's advice, Coppola, who admitted that 'I know nothing about dancing', took over the staging of the numbers himself, sometimes asking the cast to 'move to the music' while he directed them from behind the camera. In fact, he seems to have choreographed the camera rather more than the dancers, using rapid montage to give the numbers a rhythm and structure they did not intrinsically possess. The result is incessant helicopter shots, high-angle crane shots, someone singing on the hood of a truck, others on horseback – anything, it seems, to distract from actual singing and dancing. Only in 'How Are Things in Glocca Morra?' does he allow Petula Clark to sing without too many frantic visual diversions.

Also distracting is the poor way in which the singing voices are synchronised, with added sound effects like the splashing of water, and people shrieking and laughing. 'Technically he was always trying to change the way the sound was being picked up, and had to redo a lot of it,' Astaire complained.

Finian's Rainbow was not a happy experience, but Coppola brought it in for under $4 million, which surprised the studio moguls. Warners then blew up the original 35mm to 70mm, going from a normal screen ratio to a wide-screen ratio, which meant they had to crop the top and bottom of the screen. The disastrous consequence was that, in the few scenes where Astaire danced, his feet couldn't be seen. However, the dancing of the sixty-eight-year-old Astaire, who called his last musical a 'disappointment', was limited in its scope in the rather ill-paced routines, and it was the first time in thirty-five years that inset shots of his dancing feet were used. In his one solo, 'When the Idle Poor Become The Idle Rich', there are thirteen shots in the two-minute number, and Astaire is irritatingly prevented from dancing by having to climb ladders and pile up boxes. The film, as a whole, at 144 minutes, overstayed its welcome by about an hour.

Finian's Rainbow was critically lambasted, and proved a box-office disaster. 'It was an absurd idea to take a $3.5 million musical and send it out to compete with fucking *Funny Girl* where they had rehearsed the musical numbers for two months!' Coppola commented. Before *Finian's Rainbow* was released, Warners, who had predicted a hit, offered Coppola $400,000 to make *Mame*, another musical. But by then he was determined to return to the kind of small film-making over which he would have control.

Among the few good things to come out of *Finian's Rainbow* was that Coppola met George Lucas during the production. Lucas, a skinny, bearded twenty-two-year-old in T-shirt and sneakers, was a film student at the University of Southern California. A few months earlier his student short *THX 1138:4EB (Electronic Labyrinth)* had won first prize in the National Student Film Festival. George and Francis liked each other immediately. 'I was like a fish out of water among all these old studio guys,' Coppola recalled. 'We were the only people on the production under forty or fifty. We both had been to film school, and we both had beards.' Coppola told Lucas that he would offer him a job on the next film he was planning, a small-scale, personal project called *The Rain People*.

6 On the Road

When we made *Rain People* we had this unusual format, a very small caravan that could strike anywhere. We began to feel like Robin Hood and his band, we really had the film-making machine in our hands and it didn't need to be in Hollywood, it could be anywhere.

In early 1968, Coppola took the plunge, abandoned his career as a screenwriter, and embarked on *The Rain People*, a project that was close to his heart. With a budget of just $750,000 from Warners, and a total fee of $50,000 to write, direct and edit, he sank his own cash into certain expensive items of equipment. 'If you're not willing to risk some money when you're young, you're certainly not going to risk anything in the years that follow,' Coppola remarked. He also managed to get a salary from Warners for George Lucas to make a documentary about the making of the film.

The source of *The Rain People* dates from his childhood when his mother, feeling that domestic pressures threatened to overwhelm her, disappeared for three days. 'She wouldn't say where she had gone. She told me she had stayed in a motel. It just clicked with me, you know. The idea of a woman just leaving and staying in a motel.'

Around 1959, for his writing class, while still under the influence of Tennessee Williams, Coppola had developed a story called *The Old Grey Station Wagon* about three wives who leave their husbands and take off across country. It was the early draft of *The Rain People*. When he later developed it, he wrote the lead with Shirley Knight in mind. He had met the thirty-year-old blonde actress at the Cannes Festival in 1967 when he was there with *You're A Big Boy Now*, and she with Anthony Harvey's *Dutchman*, in which her performance had greatly impressed Francis. Like Elizabeth Hartman, Knight had also been in *The Group*.

Having been restricted mainly to the Warners backlot on *Finian's Rainbow*, Coppola decided to film *The Rain People* during a four-month trip through eighteen states, including West Virginia, Tennessee, Kentucky and Nebraska, beginning in early April 1968. He shaved off his beard to gain respectability with the authorities in the various states, because he wanted freedom to shoot wherever he wished and to use local people to play small parts and extras. He had a large camper van with editing facilities, and the cast and crew followed in several station wagons, with which he was in constant radio communication. Eleanor followed them in a Volkswagen van with the children, staying with Francis in motels.

Coppola was happy to be able to shoot outside Hollywood with a small group of trusted colleagues, many of whom would remain faithful to him for much of his career. *The Rain People* brought together for the first time the actors James Caan and Robert Duvall, Walter Murch (sound montage), Barry Malkin (editor) and Mona Skager (production associate), as well as old friends from college Bart Patton (the axe killer in *Dementia 13*) and Ronald Colby as producers. Coppola was determined to shoot the movie like a French New Wave film with a small crew, light equipment, and improvisation as the keynote.

Lucas' film called *filmmaker: a diary by george lucas* (note the pretentious lower case lettering) describes the romantic agony of living in trailers and converted buses, arguments with unions and local authorities, and fights over the phone with the studio backing the film. However, Lucas cut out one particular acrimonious confrontation between Coppola and Shirley Knight. It was one among many personality clashes between director and star.

Like the character she was playing, Knight was pregnant. She disliked the cramped travel, she hated doing the semi-nude sex scenes, and she didn't like the way the film was going. She was the only dissenter among the 'yes men'. But there was also hidden tension among the crew. Although Francis had his wife with him, all other wives, husbands, boy- and girlfriends were barred. He even left the crew in a one-horse town while he went off to New York for a break. 'Francis was saying all the "all-for-one" stuff, and then he goes off and screws around in New York,' commented George Lucas. 'He felt he had the right to do that, and I told him it wasn't fair. We got into a big fight over it.'

Despite the problems of shooting on the road, Coppola brought in *The Rain People* on time and for $740,000. He then installed Walter Murch in a small house in Benedict Canyon with the film, a Nagra, a Moviola, and a transfer machine, and let him get on with the editing.

The cryptic title of *The Rain People* refers, according to Coppola, to those 'sad people who cry a lot over marriages that don't work.' In the film, they are described, in words inappropriately given to the simple-minded ex-footballer played by James Caan, as those people made of rain, who 'cry themselves away'. But the picture is an unsentimental view of a woman trying to find freedom from a marriage that is stifling her. Discovering she is pregnant, Natalie (Shirley Knight) decides to take off in her car and have an abortion. On the road, she picks up Kilgannon (James Caan), whom she seduces in her motel room. When 'Killer' releases thousands of chicks from their hutches at a farm where he works (a scene that echoes the moment in *Rumble Fish* when Mickey Rourke frees birds from their cages in a pet shop), she pays his fine, and takes up with Gordon, a cynical cop (Robert Duvall). When 'Killer' sees Gordon forcing his attentions on Natalie in the trailer park where they live, the two men get into a fight and Killer is accidentally shot dead. It is suggested that Natalie will return to her husband.

This sub-feminist road movie, one of the first of the genre, benefited from the manner in which Coppola chose to shoot it. The desolate small towns, the endless highways, the depressing motels and the cramped atmosphere of a trailer park give it a real sense of place. Unfortunately, Natalie is rather an unsympathetic character (as was the liberated Barbara Darling in *You're A Big Boy Now*) who, having left her nice Italian-American husband, humiliates and taunts the men she runs into on her odyssey, before submitting herself to a brutal cop. The reason she has fled her husband, is that she feels guilt about her unwillingness to fulfil her wifely obligations. 'You married an incompetent. I'm irresponsible, cruel and aimless. I hate to cook and I'm sloppy. If you really knew me, you'd hate me,' she tells her husband. In fact, Coppola could be accused of punishing Natalie, in the end, for having strayed.

But *The Rain People* was evidence that Coppola was mastering the medium with greater assurance with each film. The use of close-ups and the handling of the actors is meaningful and all three leads come over strongly despite their somewhat elliptical roles (though the over-abundance of brief flashbacks fractures the narrative). The film revealed that Coppola, like many of the European directors whom he admires – Ingmar Bergman, Alain Resnais – was prepared to explore new narrative techniques as well as new production methods.

The Rain People, a dark view of an alienated America, was not especially well received by the critics, many of whom thought it pretentious, too literary and unsubtle in its play on the emotions, while the 'cowardly' ending drew much opprobrium. However, when Coppola's name began to mean something after the success of *The Godfather*, the film was sought out and gained a faithful following.

The last credit on *The Rain People* reads: 'Produced by American Zoetrope, San Francisco'. The Greek word Zoetrope means 'life movement', but it was also the name of the 19th-century toy invented by William George Horner, which was a revolving drum with images that spun around rapidly, giving the impression of movement.

Coppola moved to San Francisco because he thought it was 'a beautiful place to live, and had an artistic, bohemian tradition . . . . We would have independence, and we'd be close enough to LA to be able to draw on talent from there . . . . The difference is that in LA people talk deals, in San Francisco they talk films.' According to Eleanor Coppola, Francis 'dreamed of this group of poets, film-makers and writers who would drink espresso on North Beach and talk of their work, and it would be good. They would publish their writing in *City* magazine, do new plays at the Little Fox Theater, and make experimental films at American Zoetrope.'

Zoetrope was officially opened on 13 December 1969, at 827 Folsom Street, a former warehouse bought by Coppola. With Coppola as president of the company, George Lucas was appointed vice-president and Mona Skager treasurer and secretary. Many people, among them Mike Nichols and Stanley Kubrick, phoned and wrote to give encouragement to the new company. One day Orson Welles called to discuss a 16mm feature he wanted to make at Zoetrope.

'A lot of things I talked about years ago are beginning to happen,' Coppola boasted. 'I'm sitting here with the means of making films with intelligent costs. I've also got good relationships with some of the more talented young film-makers around because I was the one who stuck out his neck to give them the chance. I believe in a couple of years we'll be far bigger and more important than any two Hollywood studios put together.'

Zoetrope was well equipped with a range of cameras: Arriflex 35mm, Eclair 35mm, 16mm, and Super 8mm; Nagra portable sound recorders, and soundproofed editing rooms with advanced Steenbeck and Keller (KEM) editing machines. The Keller sound system could record, play back, mix and transfer sound from any one of seven strips of film to any other, and run that sound in sync with any image from 70mm down to Super-8 and video. Unfortunately, when it broke down a repair man had to come all the way from Germany. Yet Coppola still felt small was beautiful, and relished the idea of making inexpensive movies, some even with a 16mm camera.

When Zoetrope produced George Lucas' first feature, *THX-1138* (starring Robert Duvall), it was made in Techniscope, an inexpensive widescreen process that uses standard 35mm film and a specially modified camera to produce wide-screen aspect ratio while cutting film and processing costs in half. The small-scale Orwellian sci-fi film, which was shot in San Francisco's then unfinished subway system, was hated by Warners and only released in 1971, when it earned a disappointing one million dollars in rentals.

Meanwhile, *The Rain People* made no money, and Warners withdrew their support from Zoetrope. 'It looked as though we would never make another movie again,' said Lucas. Coppola's idealistic dream of making American Zoetrope into a viable alternative to the Hollywood studios was shattered.

'Zoetrope was picked clean. Everyone had used it, no one had contributed, and there was a time when I was literally staving off the sheriff from putting the chain across the door,' Coppola recalled. Then, out of the blue, Coppola was made an offer he could not refuse.

7 Family Values

The success of *The Godfather* went to my head like a rush of perfume. I thought I couldn't do anything wrong.

Around October 1970, Robert Evans, vice-president in charge of production at Paramount, contacted Coppola about directing the screen version of Mario Puzo's bestseller, *The Godfather*. They had already offered it to a number of directors, among them, Peter Yates, John Frankenheimer and Costa-Gavras, all of whom refused because they felt the book glamorized the mob. The astute Evans said he chose Coppola because he was the only Italian director in Hollywood. 'When I hired Francis for *The Godfather* everybody thought I was nuts . . . but I had faith in him. He knew the way these men ate their food, kissed each other, talked. He knew the grit.' There were other reasons. Paramount needed a hungry young director who would work for relatively little salary, who could shoot fast and inexpensively, and whose Italian name might pacify the Italian lobby who felt the subject was demeaning to their people.

But, as remembered by Evans, 'There was one problem. He didn't want to do it. He couldn't get a cartoon made in town, yet he didn't want to make *The Godfather*. To his credit, his convictions were strong in not wanting to immortalize the families that blackened his Italian heritage. Here I am, on my knees begging the director who had made three features [four-and-a-half, actually] all flops, to please, please put *The Godfather* on screen.'

Coppola eventually agreed to make it, but on one condition: he would make it, not as a film about organized gangsters, but as a family chronicle. Paramount agreed, and gave him $150,000 for writing and directing the picture and seven-and-a-half per cent of the net profits. It was thought that Coppola would have given much of his salary to get Zoetrope out of debt, but instead he bought a twenty-eight-room turn-of-the-century Queen Anne house, high on Pacific Heights, with turrets, stained-glass windows, and a spectacular view of the Bay and Golden Gate Bridge.

Before shooting on *The Godfather* began, the Italian-American Civil Rights League threatened to stop or picket the film until they were assured that neither the word Mafia nor Cosa Nostra was to be used in the film. They were reassured by the name of Coppola as director, and the fact that, according to the producer Albert Ruddy, 'It's the Jewish producer who's defamed and an Irish cop', not Italian-Americans.

Then there was the problem of casting. Paramount insisted on a big WASP star like Robert Redford, Warren Beatty, Jack Nicholson or Ryan O'Neal for the key role of Michael Corleone. Coppola wanted Al Pacino. The thirty-one-year-old actor had only made two films previously, but his role as the psychologically disturbed drug addict and dealer in Jerry Schatzberg's *Panic in Needle Park* (1971) had attracted Coppola's attention. Pacino had to be given three screen tests, during which he was intensely nervous and forgot his lines, inprovising terrible dialogue to cover up. But Coppola got his own way against Robert Evans' wishes. Coppola said, 'I want Pacino, and I'm the director! You won't use him, I'm quitting this fuckin' picture!' Evans replied, 'Okay, I'll use the midget.'

Then Francis said he wanted Marlon Brando for the title role. Evans was dismissive: 'Sonny Tufts, Troy Donahue, Tab Hunter, Fabian – put them all together – Marlon Brando was colder.' Italian producer Dino De Laurentiis said, 'If Brando plays the Don, forget opening the film in Italy. They'd laugh him off the screen.'

Stanley Jaffe said, 'As President of Paramount Pictures, I assure you that Marlon Brando will never appear in this motion picture, and furthermore, as President of the company, I will no longer allow you to discuss it.' Nevertheless, Coppola continued to plead for Brando, saying he was the only actor with the charisma to play it. When Jaffe refused once again, Coppola jumped up and down and then started hyperventilating, clutched his stomach and collapsed on the floor. Jaffe was intimidated into finally giving in. Brando took only $100,000 and a percentage of the film, which eventually yielded $16 million.

Initially, the budget on the film was a mere $2 million, the executives rejecting the idea of a period piece as being too expensive. They were eventually convinced to raise the budget by producer Albert Ruddy, backed up by Coppola, when it was decided that the film had to be set in the immediate post-war period, using authentic 1940s automobiles and costumes to create the background that lends so much to the atmosphere of the movie. An important addition to Coppola's team was the production designer Dean Tavoularis, who was to establish a 'look' to almost every one of Coppola's subsequent films.

'The whole visual style was laid out before we ever shot one foot of film,' recalled Coppola. We [Francis, Tavoularis, cinematographer Gordon Willis] talked about the contrast between good and evil, light and

dark. How we'd really use darkness, how we'd start out with a black sheet
of paper and paint in the light, and the camera would never move.'

On 29 March 1971, the camera started to roll on *The Godfather*. A few weeks
later, 20th Century-Fox's *Patton*, one of the three biggest money-makers of
1970, won Francis a screenwriting Oscar, which he shared with Edmund
North who had 'restructured' his script and whom he had never met.

Much of *The Godfather* was shot on location in Hollywood, Las Vegas
and New York. But all was not well. Evans considered the rushes so bad
that he contemplated replacing Coppola with Elia Kazan until Brando
threatened to quit the film if Francis was fired. 'Brando saved my neck,'
Coppola acknowledged. However, pressure continued to be placed on
him every day.

The cinematographer Gordon Willis walked off the set more than once
in protest at what he saw as Coppola's incompetence. The director later
explained: 'I agreed with Gordy [Willis] on how it should look – no zoom
shots, and grainy, like old period photographs. But he hates and misuses
actors. He wants them to hit marks. I said no. They're not mechanics.
They're artists.' Willis maintained that he and Francis had agreed that it
should be a tableau movie, with the actors moving in and out of frame,
giving it the feel of a 1940s picture. 'Francis wasn't well schooled in that
kind of moviemaking,' Willis recalled. 'He'd done some on-the-road
running-around kinda stuff. You can't shoot a classic movie like video
theatre.' Coppola and Willis resolved their differences, the latter
returned to shoot the film at the one hundred and two New York locations,
and spent two weeks with Pacino and a group of Italian actors in
Taormina, Sicily. A village was found to represent the small town of
Corleone, which actually exists near Palermo and on which Mario Puzo
based his novel.

During the shooting, there were rumours that Coppola's sister, Talia
Shire, who played Brando's daughter, was giving a poor performance.
Actually, Francis thought Talia too pretty for the part. 'A guy who's going
to marry into a Mafia family has to have a fat little dumpy Italian girl with
an ugly face. Tallie is wrong. She's got to go!' he exclaimed. But just as
he was about to fire her, his mother, Italia, begged him to keep her on. In
fact, Talia gives a poignant portrayal of a battered wife still clinging to
her husband, and brings power to the scene when she destroys china and
furniture in the house because of his philandering.

Apart from his sister, Eleanor, Roman and Gian-Carlo are featured in
the baptism scene in which the Coppola's newly-born third child, Sofia,
is the baby. Italia appeared as a switchboard operator, and Carmine is
seen playing the piano. The latter also wrote additional music to the Nino
Rota score, most of which was used in the opening wedding scene.

The slaughter of Sonny (James Caan) at the toll-booths was shot over three days on a deserted airstrip at Floyd Bennett Field, which was dressed up to look like a highway. The scene where Brando is almost assassinated while buying fruit was filmed on Mott Street in Little Italy, though Coppola had to take down all the television aerials. For three days, crowds watched Brando choosing fruit and then being gunned down.

Over a month into the shoot, Coppola called in Robert Towne. Towne had written for Roger Corman, and had been special script consultant on *Bonnie and Clyde* (1967). He was asked to help with the final scene between Michael Corleone and his father, where the Don warns his son to 'trust no one' and transfers power from one generation to the next. The death of Don Corleone – one of the best scenes in the movie – came out of improvisation by Brando. He suggested he make fangs out of a piece of orange peel when he is playing with his grandson in the garden, pretending to frighten the boy. When he collapses, the child laughs thinking he is playing a game. The funeral follows immediately afterwards, avoiding any conventional deathbed scene.

Marlon Brando at forty-seven was much too young for the ageing Mafia don. The make-up expert Dick Smith solved this problem by adding wrinkles to Brando's skin with liquid latex, especially around the eyes and nose. A special denture was inserted along his lower jawline which jutted the actor's jaw. His cheeks were then stuffed with a gummy substance to effect heavy jowls, a device that gave rise to rumours that Brando spent hours stuffing his cheeks with cottonwool and newspapers. To give the impression that he was hard of hearing, Brando wore ear-plugs, which actually gave him difficulty in catching the other actors' lines; he wore padding to give him a paunch and weights attached to his feet to achieve the heavy walk of an overweight, elderly man.

In October 1971, Coppola returned to San Francisco with 500,000 feet of footage, more than ninety hours of film. It was edited down to two-and-a-half hours. When Robert Evans saw the edited version, he told Coppola to make it longer. 'The fat fuck shot a great film, but it ain't on the screen,' Evans commented. He got Coppola to make it 175 minutes, a wise decision as it turned out.

The saga of the Corleones, a powerful family within a group of families in the Mafia, needs the breathing space to develop the intricacies of the plot and characters as it builds up a rich pattern of relationships, meticulously detailing the rituals of an enclosed group. An objective viewpoint is attempted by using the outsider Kay (Diane Keaton, in her second film), to whom the complicated relationships within the family are explained, serving to inform audiences at the same time.

From the very opening, when a minor character in close-up says 'I believe in America . . .', a certain ironic note is struck. The wedding sequence stresses the irony of the situation as it moves between the joyous al fresco celebration of mafia chief Don Corleone's daughter, and the Don's shuttered room in the estate where he is receiving supplicants who want him to 'deal with' their enemies. Towards the end of the film, the action cuts back and forth between the christening at a church and a series of brutal murders. Coppola also uses tunes such as 'Have Yourself a Merry Little Christmas' to point out the contrasts between the violence and normal life. Most of all, the film stresses the link between the Mafia and American capitalism. As Brando said in a *Newsweek* interview, 'In a way the Mafia is the best example of capitalists we have. Don Corleone is just an ordinary business magnate who is trying to do the best he can for the group he represents and for his family.'

Coppola controls the material in a masterful manner, as in the way he builds up the tension when Michael meets the rival gangster Sollozo (Al Lettieri) and McCluskey (Sterling Hayden), a crooked policeman, in a small remote Italian restaurant, with the aim of killing them both. The excessive violence is justified by the plot and is never arbitrary. However, audiences seemed to have been more shocked by the scene when Hollywood tycoon Jack Woltz (John Marley) wakes up to find the bloody head of his prize racehorse in the sheets beside him, than by the killing of fellow human beings. Incidentally, the horse had been killed by a dog food company, and the head was packed in dry ice and delivered to the film set. (In *Apocalypse Now*, Martin Sheen wakes up with a human head in his lap.)

Especially outstanding was the casting of the film, right down to the smallest role. The hulking ex-wrestler Lenny Montana, a non-professional actor, who plays one of the Don's henchman, couldn't remember his lines when he comes to offer his services to Brando at the wedding. Coppola used his hesitancy by writing Montana a scene in which he rehearses what he is going to say, and then forgets when faced with the Don.

Brando creates an iconographic figure: the throaty voice, the hand gestures so often reminiscent of the Pope, his weeping over the corpse of his eldest son, a tear on his cheek when Michael greets him; and then the switch to his stern position as a godfather, but playfully entertaining his little grandson even as he is dying. James Caan (in life the son of a Jewish kosher meat dealer) has all the right Italian gestures and is perfect as the hedonistic volatile Sonny, heir apparent to the Corleone family, but whose bloody ways end in his own death. Robert Duvall, as Tom Hagen, the sharp lawyer, confidante and adopted son of the family, gives a strong, discreet performance, holding the family and, indeed, the film together. Of Sicilian descent, Al Pacino, looking younger than his thirty-one years, moves gradually from being the wide-eyed and bashful youngest brother, to controlled coldness and deadpan calculation which he puts to bloody use in the service of the family. The film ends with Pacino taking over the reins of power, almost as if Coppola was conscious that a second *Godfather* would be made.

The Godfather opened on 11 March 1972, and became one of the biggest box-office successes ever. But Coppola stuck to his ideal. 'My dream of dreams was that *The Godfather* would net me one million dollars, and that, conservatively invested, could bring around fifty thousand dollars, and with that coming in I could spend all my time writing my own stuff, without the interruption of having to deal with studios.' He came close to that dream with his next film.

8 Bugging the Bugger

I was fascinated to learn that bugging was a profession, not just some private cop going out and eavesdropping with primitive equipment.

Francis Coppola made it clear that, despite the success of *The Godfather*, it was 'fundamentally just a gangster movie', and he therefore wished to re-establish his reputation as a serious artist. At the time of the opening of *The Godfather*, he had many opportunities to do so. He was hired by Robert Evans to work on the script of *The Great Gatsby* because the existing script by Truman Capote was found to be unsatisfactory; he directed a stage production of Noël Coward's *Private Lives* in San Francisco for the American Conservatory Theater, followed by Gottfried von Einem's *The Visit of the Old Lady* for the San Francisco opera.

Coppola was also executive producer of George Lucas' second feature, *American Grafitti*, the success of which gained the director enough money to make *Star Wars*. (Incidentally, the film one sees showing in the local movie theatre with *American Grafitti* is *Dementia 13*.) Along with Peter Bogdanovich and William Friedkin, Coppola formed The Director's Company, for which, it was hoped, each would direct two films, and produce a third by one of the others, all of them to be released by Paramount. In the event, Bogdanovich's *Paper Moon* and *Daisy Miller*, and Coppola's *The Conversation* were the only three that appeared under that banner.

It was in 1967 that Coppola developed the idea for a film about a sound surveillance expert, based to some extent on Hal Lipset, the sound wizard who had been summoned from San Francisco to analyse the eighteen-minute 'blank' section of White House tape during the Watergate investigations. 'The movie will say something significant about the nightmarish situation that has developed in our society,' Coppola told the *New York Times*. 'A system that employs all the sophisticated electronic tools that are available to intrude upon our private lives.'

Among the influences on *The Conversation* were Michelangelo Antonioni's *Blow-Up* (a photographer tries to make sense of a picture as

Coppola's wiretapper puzzles over different snatches of conversation), and Herman Hesse's then fashionable novel *Steppenwolf*, the lonely hero of which, Harry Haller, resembles Coppola's Harry Caul, with whom Francis identified. 'In the scene where he's in the park [in a dream sequence], and tells all that stuff about his childhood and the polio – those are things that actually happened to me . . . . I think his roots are roots of guilt. Ever since he was a little kid, everything that has happened he has in some way been responsible for . . . .'

Coppola had originally thought of Marlon Brando for the role, probably in his *Last Tango in Paris* 'angst' mode, but the actor expressed no interest. He then cast forty-three-year-old Gene Hackman, who had just become a star in Friedkin's *The French Connection*. Coppola explained: 'Hackman is ideal for the part because he's so ordinary, so unexceptional in appearance . . . . He's just a businessman.' But when Hackman arrived on set looking spruce and handsome, exactly the wrong look for the character of Harry Caul, Coppola got him to cut his hair so he'd look bald, and with ageing make-up, spectacles and a small moustache gradually transformed him into the 'lonely and anonymous' protagonist.

Shooting on *The Conversation* started in San Francisco on 26 November 1972. Many of the scenes Coppola had written were technically very difficult to shoot; the master set-up in Union Square, for example, required four camera crews and six cameras working simultaneously, plus many sound technicians. To get the effect he needed, Coppola pointed out the actors to the cameramen and told them, 'Try to find them and keep them in focus.' Then he had the actors walk through the action again and again, surrounded by real passers-by who had no idea a movie was being shot. The actors themselves never knew whether the cameras were rolling or not. Some of the sound men were so well camouflaged that they were arrested by armed policemen, who thought they might be snipers trying to kill Coppola.

A month into the shoot, there was a difference of opinion between the experienced cinematographer Haskell Wexler and Dean Tavoularis, the production designer. Wexler objected to certain locations that he thought would be too difficult to shoot. Although Wexler and Coppola were friends, the latter sided with Tavoularis, feeling that the cinematographer was forcing him to make a different film.

As a result, Coppola had to close down the shoot for ten days, before bringing in Bill Butler, the lighting cameraman on *The Rain People*, as cinematographer. During the break, Coppola watched *The Conformist* every day for inspiration. Although Bernardo Bertolucci's ironic and stylish study of pre-war Italy bears little obvious relation to Coppola's intriguing post-Watergate thriller, it does follow the workings of an isolated man.

The tricky editing took almost a year to complete. Walter Murch, who got the credit of 'supervising editor, sound montage and re-recording', was given almost a free hand to mix and edit it. However, Murch had difficulties because of script problems. The ending had always been a bit vague, and he had to keep taking it apart and putting it together again, inventing new plot constructions and rediscovering others, almost like Harry Caul in the film. With the help of brilliant sound montages it began to work, and was resolved by a sonic clue based on the interpretation of the line, 'He'd kill us if he got the chance.'

In *The Conversation*, Coppola gives us access to the protagonist's state of mind through his behaviour, speech and dreams. Gene Hackman as 'the best bugger on the West Coast', reveals Harry Caul in all his complexity, without a hint of affectation or sentimentality. An intensely lonely and private man, Caul tries to remain emotionally detached from the people on whom he is eavesdropping. Like Michael Corleone in *The Godfather* trilogy, he does his job coldly – a professional distancing himself from his victims – although both characters, being Catholics, have need of the confessional and redemption.

After taping a conversation between two young people in a crowded square, which gives him three imperfect recordings of the dialogue, Harry is convinced that a death may result from it, and refuses to hand in the tapes to his client (Robert Duvall in an uncredited cameo). Gradually, he finds that he himself is being bugged, and he becomes more and more paranoid, wrecking his whole apartment, even smashing a Virgin Mary statuette, to find a microphone.

The film, although shot in San Francisco, eschews all the locations with which moviegoers are familiar, going for impersonal apartments, office blocks, hotels and a stark underground studio where Harry works. These choices create a background of concealed menace, where everybody and everything seems suspect. Towards the end, the methodical style – people moving in and out of frame, leaving empty spaces; lengthy wordless sequences – is interrupted by Harry's surreal dreams of a bloody murder which he cannot prevent, so that the film moves edgily from the physical to the metaphysical, from the objective to the subjective.

By March 1973, *The Conversation* was in the can. In the same month, Coppola was in Los Angeles for the Academy Award presentations. *The Godfather*, which was nominated for eleven Oscars, eventually won three: Best Picture, Best Actor (Brando) and Best Screenplay (Coppola and Mario Puzo). Brando sent a Native American, Sacheen Littlefeather, to refuse the award on his behalf, reading excerpts of a letter from the actor complaining about America's treatment of Native American people.

Gene Hackman in The Conversation **(1974).**

With the money from *The Godfather* and *American Graffiti*, Zoetrope was more than solvent again. Coppola bought another property at the edge of Chinatown called Columbus Tower to house the company, and he bought City magazine. However, although *The Conversation* won the Palme d'Or at Cannes in May 1974, it failed to get an audience. It was his seventh feature (counting *Tonight For Sure*) as director and, so far, the only commercial success he had had was *The Godfather*, to which he now reluctantly returned.

9 Extended Family Values

> I was fascinated by the idea of a movie that would work freely in time, that would go both forward and backward in time. I felt that *The Godfather* had never been finished; morally I believed that the Family would be destroyed, and it would be like a kind of Götterdammerung.

The huge success of *The Godfather* gave Coppola almost carte blanche on the sequel, though Francis made it clear that *The Godfather Part II* would not be the 'usual cheap imitation of its parent . . . in order to squeeze more money out of it. I thought it would be exciting if I could reverse that: make a film that was more ambitious, more beautiful, more advanced than the first.'

Because of his position *vis-à-vis* Paramount, Coppola asked for and got a million dollars plus thirteen per cent of the studio's gross rental profits. Paramount also gave in to his demands that he produce as well as direct, all of which allowed him the freedom and the money to do what he wanted.

The casting was already fixed from *Part I*. Al Pacino, who was growing in fame, and who had just completed Sidney Lumet's *Serpico*, was offered twenty times the salary he had received for the first film, but he hated the script. Coppola, therefore, rewrote all of Michael Corleone's scenes in three days.

Paramount wanted Brando to reappear as Vito Corleone's younger self, but he wanted far too much money. So there was the question of who would play the Don in the 'prequel' section. Both Jack Nicholson and Dustin Hoffman were considered, but after seeing thirty-year-old Robert De Niro as a loud-mouthed small-time hustler in Martin Scorsese's *Mean Streets*, Coppola thought he would be just right. He also tended, where possible, to cast actors of Italian descent. In fact, De Niro had spent hours in his youth studying Brando, and was able to recreate the older star's stiff formal postures and measured gestures, the calm behind the eyes, and the husky, quietly convincing voice. However, De Niro admitted to feeling intimidated by a role that had Brando's stamp on it.

The Corleone family: papa Vito (Robert De Niro), mama (Francesca deSapio) and little Sonny, Connie, Fredo and Michael in The Godfather Part II **(1974).**

Eleanor and the three children joined Francis on location at Lake Tahoe, where the sets for Michael Corleone's family estate were constructed at the lavish Fleur de Lac estate built by millionaire Henry Kaiser in 1934. The Coppola family were crammed into a bungalow for six weeks, during which time Eleanor said she never stopped crying. Francis was plagued with doubts about his career as tensions mounted at home and on the set. Pacino constantly complained about the length of the shoot, reminding Coppola that 'Lumet shot *Serpico* in eighteen days!' He also complained about Coppola's handling of the actors. 'I go up to Francis, I've got a problem I want to talk to him about. So what does he do? He tells me his problems. What do I want to hear his problems for? He's the director!'

From Lake Tahoe, the crew moved on to the Dominican Republic in order to film the Havana sequences. When the seventy-four-year-old Lee Strasberg, playing the crime syndicate treasurer Hyman Roth, fell ill during the shoot, Coppola adjusted the screenplay to make the character an ailing man. The exhausted Pacino came down with pneumonia and took three weeks to recuperate, so Coppola had to shoot around him. Fortunately, Pacino was not needed for most of the rest of the film, which involved Vito Corleone's coming to America.

From the Dominican Republic, the team moved on to Taormina for the Sicilian sequences, and the old fish market in Trieste served as a replica of the Ellis Island building. Finally, back in the USA, Dean Tavoularis had transformed New York's 6th Street into Little Italy, Manhattan, *circa* 1918.

On his return to San Francisco, Coppola had to get the film down to a watchable length. At the same time, as he had been desperately over-eating during the nine-month shoot, he had to lose some of his now two hundred and thirty-nine pounds weight. This he tried to do by fasting every Monday, though beware anyone who provoked his wrath during those days. Eventually, he had a five-hour rough cut of *The Godfather Part II*. By November 1974, he had got it down to three hours and twenty minutes, having had to sacrifice scenes that were dear to his heart, including one where Enrico Caruso arrives in Little Italy and sings 'Over There'.

The scope of *The Godfather Part II* is far more expansive than that of its predecessor. It covers many more locations and characters and deepens the Shakespearean elements in the plot. It is 1958, and Michael Corleone (Pacino) now runs his Mafia empire from his vast Lake Tahoe estate. After an assassination attempt is made on the family, Michael travels to Havana to meet gambling racketeer Hyman Roth (a compelling Strasberg), who he believes is behind the attempt. In a cold and calculating manner, Michael continues to order the murder of his enemies, including his own weak brother Fredo (John Cazale), who has betrayed

Coppola and Pacino on the set of The Godfather Part II.

him. Concurrently, the story of Michael's father, Vito Corleone (De Niro) is told in flashback, showing how he came from Sicily to settle in New York's Little Italy, and how he established himself as a powerful don.

In placing two separate narratives side by side, only touching tangentially, Coppola is able to penetrate the psychology of the members of the Corleone family, while continuing to offer an objective, critical viewpoint – as in the first film – through the character of Kay (Diane Keaton), Michael's wife. The scenes in Sicily, Vito's arrival in America as a child at the turn-of-the-century, and his subsequent fight for survival, give the story an historical context. From the shots of the immigrants' first view of the Statue of Liberty, their faces lighting up with hope, to the irony of the little boy seeing the symbolic monument again through his barred room on Ellis Island where he must remain in quarantine for three months, to the bustling dog-eat-dog life of the streets of Little Italy, the period atmosphere is brilliantly conveyed.

The camera in these scenes is more animated, especially in one of those *morceau de bravure* that adorn the saga: during a fiesta, Vito climbs over the roofs to get into the house of the local Mafia boss who he is about to kill, and the subsequent sound of the gun is drowned by the noise of fireworks in the street.

Switching to Vito's son, Michael, we see how the family has become part of America's powerful élite, with politicians and businessmen on their payroll. 'We're both part of the same hypocrisy,' Michael tells a senator, whom he later blackmails to do his bidding. The meetings in Cuba between large US corporations, gambling syndicates and the corrupt regime on the eve of the Revolution, pointedly underline the link between the Mafia and American society as a whole. Gradually, the personal tragedy of Michael takes over as he struggles to keep his wife and children, finding that, like Macbeth, he is 'in blood stepp'd in so far that, should I wade no more, returning were as tedious as go o'er.' This is conveyed superbly by Pacino, mournful, cold, calculating, soft-spoken, with sudden dangerous bursts of anger. Like *Part I*, the film ends in a series of deaths, including that of Michael's brother Fredo, shot in a fishing boat as he intones Hail Marys, hinting at redemption which would be the main theme of *Part III*.

The Godfather Part II brought Coppola three more Oscars to add to the two he already had: as producer of the Best Film, for its direction, and for writing the Best Screenplay Adaptation (with Mario Puzo). Added to this, Francis had the joy of seeing his father share with Nino Rota the Oscar for Best Original Dramatic Score. When Carmine collected his award, he said, 'If it wasn't for Francis Coppola I wouldn't be here tonight. However, if it wasn't for me, he wouldn't be here.' Italia, who wasn't mentioned, said to Coppola Sr after his speech, 'Gee, Carmine, you did a great job. I hope the labour pains weren't too bad.' Talia, who had been nominated for Best Supporting Actress, was upset not to have won. (The award went to Ingrid Bergman for *Murder On The Orient Express*.)

The success of the film *The Godfather Part II* placed Coppola in an even more enviable position than the first part of the Mafia saga had done. The Coppolas became among San Francisco's most celebrated hosts, throwing huge parties for famous visitors. With the money that was pouring in, Francis bought a fifteen-hundred-acre Napa Valley wine estate, situated near the town of Rutherford, a ninety-minute drive northeast of San Francisco, which he would use as a country retreat. On the estate stands a three-storeyed gabled Georgian-style manor, and a one-hundred-and-twenty-five-acre vineyard. Less than a year later, Coppola would be fighting for survival in the jungles of the Philippines.

10 Heart of Darkness

My film is not a movie; it's not about Vietnam. It *is* Vietnam. It's what it was really like; it was crazy. We were in the jungle, there were too many of us, we had access to too much money, too much equipment; and little by little, we went insane.

The title of Coppola's Vietnam movie to end all Vietnam movies, *Apocalypse Now*, came from 'Nirvana Now', a drug-related slogan on a hippie badge of the 1960s. Several people claimed to have first thought of re-situating (from the Congo) and updating Joseph Conrad's 1902 short novel, *Heart of Darkness*, for the screen. Coppola's colleague Carole Ballard (later to direct *The Black Stallion*) claimed to have suggested it in 1967. However, the main inspiration was an article by Michael Herr called 'The Battle for Khe San', which referred to the whole drugs, violence and rock 'n' roll ethos of the American soldiers in Vietnam.

The film was initially to be shot by George Lucas on 16 mm, using newsreel footage and a cast of unknowns, at a cost of about $1.5 million. But Lucas was now busy on a different kind of war . . . in the galaxy. Coppola then asked John Milius, who had written a screenplay in 1969, based on the Vietnam experiences of a friend of his, to direct for the same small fee, twenty-five thousand dollars, and ten per cent of the profits. But Milius had just had a success with *The Wind and the Lion* and was moving on to other projects. Thus Coppola came to direct and produce it himself, on a grand scale, using the Milius screenplay.

He had originally considered filming in Cuba, where the two *Godfather* films were popular. He did go to Havana to meet Castro, and when he returned to the USA, Francis wrote Castro a letter, which he decided not to post. It read, 'Dear Fidel, I love you . . . . We have the same initials. We both have beards. We both have power and want to use it for good purposes . . . .'

But Coppola decided on the Philippines as a better stand-in for Vietnam, particularly since President Marcos promised to put his army and airforce at his disposal, as well as providing M16 rifles and explosives, all for a vast undisclosed sum.

Coppola seen briefly as a TV director, filming the battle on the beach in Apocalypse Now **(1979), shot in the Philippines.**

As always, casting caused the first headache. Steve McQueen wanted $3 million to play Willard, then said he would play Kurtz. But when he learned that most of it was to be filmed in the Philippines over seventeen weeks, he refused. Al Pacino also turned down the Willard role, because he feared for his health after he had been ill in San Domingo. Jack Nicholson didn't have time to play Willard and didn't want the role of Kurtz. Robert Redford was taking a long vacation, and James Caan's wife was pregnant and didn't want to go to the Philippines. Coppola then thought he would not use stars at all, but the studio refused to go that route. By early 1976, Coppola had persuaded Brando to play Kurtz for $3.5 million for a month's work on location in September 1976, because Marlon wanted to enjoy the summer with his family on the South Seas atoll. Harvey Keitel, who had made such an impact in *Mean Streets* with Robert De Niro, was finally chosen to play Willard.

On 1 March 1976, Coppola flew to Manila with his wife, three children (Gio, now twelve, ten-year-old Roman, and Sofia, four), his nephew Marc, August's eldest son, who worked as a production assistant, his projectionist, a housekeeper and a babysitter. They settled in a large rented house, in the grounds of which they built a swimming pool.

Filming began less than three weeks after their arrival, but within the first days there were already problems. Keitel hated the jungle, the snakes, the heat and the insects. At the same time, Coppola was disappointed by Keitel's characterization of Willard, because 'he found it difficult to play him as a passive onlooker.' After viewing the rushes, Coppola flew back to Los Angeles and replaced Keitel with Martin Sheen, who had been so striking as the psychotic teenager in Terrence Malick's *Badlands*. Sheen, who was in the midst of shooting *The Cassandra Crossing* in Rome, flew in to Los Angeles to meet Coppola and collect the script. Francis didn't tell Keitel of his sacking direct but phoned his agent instead.

Back in the Philippines, Coppola found the logistics were hard to control. For the sequence when F5 jets had to scream over the jungle releasing canisters that look like napalm, special effects teams below had to ignite a vast fuel conflagration at precisely the right moment. In another sequence, Francis explained: 'I had fifteen helicopters up in the sky and no way to tell them if they didn't fly another ten feet they wouldn't be in the picture.' Seventy huts comprising the target were constructed at a coconut plantation. Coppola directed the attack, which consisted of four hundred and fifty actors, extras and technicians, from one of the helicopters. It went out of control and the film's paint and prop shop was hit. To make matters worse, a civil war broke out in the country, temporarily depriving Coppola of the helicopters he needed.

Nature also took a hand in making things difficult. When Robert Duvall and co were shooting the surfing sequence, they had to get out of the water quickly because sharks started to move in. (Coppola himself can be seen directing as part of a TV news team on the beach.) On 26 May, the production had to be shut down because Hurricane Olga had wrecked the huge sets. Forty inches of rain fell in six days, the Coppola's house was flooded, and many of the crew were trapped in their houses for days.

In June, Coppola flew back to the USA. The film was already six weeks behind schedule and $2 million over budget. Aside from the natural disasters, there were other contributory factors to the expense, such as the twelve hundred gallons of gasoline that had been burnt in ninety seconds for a bombing scene. When Francis decided to give himself a big thirty-seventh birthday party in the jungle, he had a six-by-eight foot cake flown in from the States. The cinematographer Vittorio Storaro and his Italian crew had fresh pasta constantly brought from Italy.

The delay caused by the tropical storm gave Coppola time to rework John Milius' script, particularly the ending. 'I didn't want to have just the typical John Milius ending, when the NVA attack and there's a gigantic battle scene, and Kurtz and Willard are fighting side by side and Kurtz gets killed, etc. etc. That's the way it was in the script. I wanted to explore the moral side.' This was to prove one of the most difficult parts of the film to resolve.

Back in Manila, Coppola was worried about Martin Sheen's performance, thinking it too bland. One hot August evening, Francis decided to get Sheen dead drunk to find 'another side of the guy', while prodding him to get deeper and deeper into the role. It worked. Next day, Sheen got into the role so deeply that in the opening hotel-room sequence he smashed his hand through a mirror, causing it to bleed badly, while the camera kept turning.

In September, Marlon Brando arrived in Manila, much overweight despite having submitted to a crash diet in an LA clinic. To make the character of Kurtz look mythic, Coppola used a giant double for the long shots, avoiding Brando's obesity as much as possible.

I thought it was an idiotic script [Brando later commented] but I didn't say this to Francis. In such situations I've found it's best to say, 'This may be all right the way you're going to do it, but I think we're missing a bet by not changing it.' Without informing Francis I shaved my head, found some black clothing and asked the cameraman and lighting crew to photograph me under electric lighting while I spoke half in darkness with a disembodied voice . . . . I was good at bullshitting Francis and persuading him to think my way, and he bought it . . . .

Brando spent hours discussing his role with the director, while Dennis Hopper, high on drugs, improvised as best he could. Coppola snatched a few hours of sleep each night at the Pagsanjan Rapids Hotel, close to the location where the scenes of Kurtz's compound were staged and photographed, trying to work out a satisfactory ending. As the shooting continued endlessly, and as problems mounted upon problems, Coppola lay on a roof in the rain, crying, 'Let me out of here. Let me just quit and go home. I can't do it. I can't see it . . . . This is like an opening night. The curtain goes up and there's no show.' On the set, he was short-tempered and screamed at everybody, an expression of the panic he was feeling.

On 5 March 1977, Sheen, who had been drinking heavily, suffered a heart attack while alone in a mountain cabin. He had to crawl for a quarter of a mile to reach help. It was decided that the flight to Manila would kill him. So serious was it, that Sheen even took the last rites from a priest who didn't speak English. He was eventually flown to a hospital in Manila, and was able to return to work on 19 April. Before that, as seen in the documentary *Hearts of Darkness* about the making of the film, Coppola yelled that Sheen's condition had been leaked to the trade papers, which could have pulled the plug on the production. 'Even if he dies,' Coppola declared, 'I don't want to hear anything but good news until it comes from me.'

Meanwhile, Coppola himself collapsed, both physically and emotionally. The film had become his own personal Vietnam, and he was turning into Kurtz. 'It is scary to watch someone you love go into the centre of himself and confront his fears, fear of failure, fear of death, fear of going insane,' Eleanor wrote. He became himself again by joining Ellie and the children for a break at Hidden Valley volcano resort where they swam in a warm mineral pool.

Refreshed, while Sheen was recovering, Coppola shot doubles in long shot, but he did cut down on some of the actor's scenes. The film was now about $15 million over the original budget, and had far exceeded the shooting schedule. For example, at the start, fourteen-year-old Larry Fishburne, who was playing a character of eighteen, was the right age by the time the film was shown. Francis had mortgaged all his personal assets (including his Napa Valley estate) as a guarantee for the $10 million loan made to him by United Artists, the distributing company, to complete the film.

On 21 May 1977, the shoot of *Apocalypse Now* finally ended. 'I've never in my life seen so many people so happy to be unemployed,' Coppola said at the wrap party. A month later, Coppola told Walter Murch he had four months to edit the film. The story line was still unclear, and even two hundred and fifty hours of footage didn't cover all the plot possibilities that might emerge during the cutting. To cover some gaps, Coppola shot some inserts and pick-ups at his Napa Valley estate.

Coppola then got Michael Herr, who had just published *Dispatches*, his brilliant reportage book on Vietnam, to come to San Francisco and write the narration. When he arrived, he found Coppola and his colleagues exhausted and depressed, staring at 1.5 million feet of film. Herr remarked that 'the narration written thus far was totally useless. So, over a period of a year I wrote various narrations, while Murch continued to experiment with sound. Thus the opening was postponed from May to October, and then again until the spring of 1979. Needless to say, the press had a field day, sensing a bomb of gigantic proportions and dubbing it 'Apocalypse When?'.

The Black Stallion, directed by Carole Ballard, which Coppola was producing for Zoetrope, was also behind schedule while money was still being poured into *Apocalypse Now*. Sneak previews were disappointing, and Coppola kept on recutting it, offering different audiences two different endings, one ending with a bang and the other with a whimper: a series of infra-red shots of explosions in long shot (the 35mm version), or Sheen leading Larry Fishburne away from Kurtz's camp (70mm version). A third alternative, an immense ground-and-air attack on the camp by American and Viet-Cong forces, was abandoned.

Notwithstanding the prevarications, Coppola decided to risk showing the film at the 1979 Cannes Film Festival, insisting that it was 'work in progress'. A quadraphonic soundtrack was produced in time, and it was entered in competition. Coppola's risk paid off, and *Apocalypse Now* shared the Golden Palm with Volker Schlöndorff's *The Tin Drum*.

Apocalypse Now follows the journey of Captain Willard (Martin Sheen), commanding a Navy patrol boat as he goes up a Vietnamese river in search of the mysterious Colonel Kurtz (Marlon Brando), who has set himself up as the god of a tribe of jungle Indians. Willard has been ordered by the CIA to 'terminate' Kurtz with 'extreme prejudice'. On the perilous trip (in both senses of the word), Willard and his young crew of 'rock 'n' rollers with one foot in the grave', come across the mad, surf-loving Colonel Kilgore (Robert Duvall), who carries out a helicopter bombing raid on a peasant village. Eventually, they reach Kurtz, and Willard reluctantly fulfils his mission. Coppola avoids showing the killing of Kurtz directly but, in the manner of Eisenstein in *The Strike*, uses the slaughter of a water buffalo as a visual metaphor. (The beast was decapitated as part of a real ceremony by Filipino tribesmen.)

Apocalypse Now assaults the senses with some extraordinary set-pieces. Coppola certainly achieved his aim of wanting to 'give its audience a sense of the horror, the madness, the sensuousness and the moral dilemma of the Vietnam War.' The opening scene is a perfect illustration of how expert Coppola is in combining vision and sound to create different levels of meaning. The sight and sound of helicopter blades dissolves into those of the blades of an electric fan on the ceiling above Martin Sheen, whose face is seen upside down, his blue eyes staring, the same eyes through which the whole insane enterprise will be seen.

The combined brilliance of the cinematography, editing and sound montage (Walter Murch), overseen by Coppola's grandiose vision (sound montage/design) makes the bombing sequence one of the most celebrated in cinema. As the helicopters move in with Wagner's 'The Ride Of The Valkyries' blasting out 'to scare the shit out of the slopes', we see the peaceful village below, the different reactions of the pilots, and the bloody aftermath, when Duvall announces, 'I love the smell of napalm in the morning. It smells like . . . victory!'

The quest for Kurtz in 'the heart of darkness' is like a nightmarish Disneyland ride which ends when we (and Willard) are forced to listen to twenty minutes of the muddled mumblings of the crazed Brando, as he quotes T. S. Eliot. But it has a kind of quiet grandeur, compared with the loud grandeur of the preceding hundred and twenty minutes or so. Brando's last words, 'The horror! The horror!', sum up the film, echoing the final utterance in *The Bridge on the River Kwai* – 'Madness! Madness!'

At last, three and a half years after it started shooting, with the initial thirteen-week schedule becoming two hundred and thirty-eight days, and the budget having risen from $12 million to $31 million, much of it coming out of Coppola's own pocket, *Apocalypse Now* opened in New York in August 1979.

Although it got mixed reviews, audiences were keen to see this phenomenon, but it would take five years to break even. In defence of the cost of the movie, Coppola said, 'I don't see why this amount shouldn't be spent on a morality story, when you can spend it on a giant gorilla, a little fairy tale like *The Wiz* or some jerk who flies up in the sky.'

In April 1980, it was nominated for eight Oscars, but won only for its sound editing and cinematography. There was a suspicion that this epic was too strong meat for the Academy. Perhaps its lack of honours could be put down to the success of Vietnam movies – *The Deer Hunter, Coming Home* – the previous year. Whatever the reasons, its maker clearly wasn't expecting to win: he didn't come to the ceremony. By that time, Coppola was digging himself further into debt and disaster.

11 Sing a Song of Millions

I'm very proud, and I imagine that years from now, just as with my other films, people will see something in it. It's an original work. It's not a copy of anything. It's a lounge operetta, pretty and sweet. I've made too many gangster and soldier movies. I like fantasy and fable.

Coppola's production company, now called Omni Zoetrope, bought the Hollywood General Studios for $5.6 million. Coppola now had a ten-and-a-half-acre lot at his disposal, with nine sound stages and thirty-four editing rooms. 'I'm trying to create a film studio that really makes sense – not a place where lawyers and businessmen make deals with independent artists. Rather, a family or a large repertory company engaged in making movies,' Francis optimistically stated.

By February 1980, Omni Zoetrope was up and running, with up to three hundred people on its books. Coppola wanted to exploit the dazzling new technological facilities that were emerging from American and Japanese laboratories, while remaining convinced that audiences wanted old-fashioned traditional genre movies. After his nightmarish experiences on *Apocalypse Now*, he announced that location shooting was a thing of the past. He called the studio his 'magical illusion device'.

British director Michael Powell was appointed 'Senior Director in Residence' in November 1980. Among the directors Coppola admired was Jean-Luc Godard whom he offered the chance to make a movie about the racketeer Bugsy Siegel. Godard expressed interest, saying that he wanted Robert de Niro and Diane Keaton to star, but it was soon abandoned. However, Coppola did get Wim Wenders, who had recently made *The American Friend*, featuring Dennis Hopper, to direct *Hammett*.

Meanwhile, Coppola started to prepare an original musical called *One From The Heart*, for which he got the four leads, Frederic Forrest, Teri Garr, Raul Julia and Nastassia Kinski, to sign contracts along the lines of the old studio deals. In order to recreate the style of the legendary Arthur Freed Unit at MGM, Coppola hired Gene Kelly as a consultant.

My brief was to pass on my knowledge of the film musical to a whole new generation of writers, directors, arrangers and choreographers [Kelly recalled]. It was the best, most effective and exciting way of passing on everything I had learned . . . Francis was very specific about the atmosphere he wanted to create. He was adamant that it should have a studio 'feel' to it. Also, it was Francis' idea to create the 'look' of the MGM musical of the Forties and Fifties – with lavish sets and production numbers etc. – a studio was an absolute essential . . . . I think Francis over-extended himself. He wanted to own the studio, run it, and take charge of all creative decisions as well. Not even Louis B. Mayer did all that . . . . Anyway, it was a terrible shame the idea didn't work out because, for the first time in twenty years, here was a man who took the musical seriously . . . .

Aside from being hampered by the unmemorable music and lyrics by Tom Waits, the reasons 'the idea didn't work out' were manifold. One of the principal problems was Coppola's over-reliance on technology. First of all, the entire screenplay was keyed onto floppy disk. Then the storyboard of some five hundred drawings was committed to video. Coppola maintained that this 'pre-visualization' gave him the opportunity to rewrite and omit certain scenes, thus reducing the editing schedule. He believed he would be able to finish shooting within six weeks.

Although the entire film was to be shot in a studio, Coppola took the actors to Las Vegas for a couple of days, where *One From The Heart* was set, using a video camera to get the sense of the real settings and atmosphere. Then they returned to LA for three weeks of technical rehearsals on the sound stages, while Dean Tavoularis supervised the final construction of the vast sets.

Coppola had the innovative idea of directing most of the film from his large Airstream trailer, just outside the sound stage. Dubbed The Silver Fish, the trailer was equipped with Sony Betamax recorders and monitors, and also contained beds, a kitchen, an espresso machine and a Jacuzzi, from where he even directed a scene. Video cameras were attached to movie cameras on the seven sound stages, so that Coppola could direct through the monitors from the trailer by remote control, his instructions coming through a loudspeaker.

This led to confusion. Cinematographer Vittorio Storaro and actress Nastassia Kinski, both of whom spoke English well, had trouble understanding what he was saying. The actors had the feeling that they were puppets in the hands of a disembodied director, who allowed little room for spontaneity. When Teri Garr was doing a nude scene, Coppola's voice was heard booming out, 'Let's see more of your boobs, turn this way, more, now turn that way . . . '. Realizing that the loudspeaker system was causing so much tension, Coppola decided to relay his directions

Gene Kelly bringing his experience of the Hollywood musical to bear on One From The Heart **(1982).**

through a floor manager with headphones, who would relay them to the performers, but it was still direction by remote control.

Gene Kelly was helping his young unknown protégé Kenny Ortega with the choreography but, as was the case between Coppola and Hermes Pan on *Finian's Rainbow*, there were clashes between the director and the famous dancer/choreographer. They had several arguments on the set, one of which involved Kelly's resistance to Coppola's demand that he choreograph a dance for Kinski in one day.

By April 1981, the film was $10 million over budget, mainly thanks to the cost of building the sets, with the neon lighting alone costing a million dollars. Coppola was forced to borrow $4 million from the Chase Manhattan bank, and Jack Singer, the Canadian financier, invested an additional $3 million in return for an undisclosed percentage of the film's gross income.

At the same time, *Hammett* was in deep trouble. Having had four screenwriters and as many versions of the script, much of it was being reshot. Michael Powell advised scrapping it, but it was too far along. *Hammett* finally surfaced at Cannes in May 1982, $10 million dollars having been spent on this inconsequential period piece.

On 15 January 1982, *One From The Heart* was shown to the public for the first time at Radio City Music Hall for two evenings, a sudden decision which took Paramount, the distributor, by surprise. The reviews were mostly devastating, Paramount withdrew and Columbia took over the distribution, giving it a decent launching, but the damage had already been done. It bombed on release.

Andrew Sarris in the *Village Voice* wrote: 'What made Coppola think that contemporary audiences were nostalgic more for the sets in the background of old movies than for the sweet sentiments in the foreground? With all his technological huffing and puffing, Coppola has thrown out the baby and photographed the bath water.' Peter Rainer in the *Los Angeles Herald Examiner* considered that: 'Coppola has misjudged his abilities as an artist. He's cast himself as a visionary – and yet his great work has been solidly grounded in the old-fashioned narrative tradition. Whenever he tried to move outside that tradition – *The Rain People*, *Apocalypse Now*, *One From The Heart* – he's foundered terribly. He's a great classical director who has disdain for classical forms.' Vincent Canby, of the *New York Times*, thought that 'as a romantic comedy [it] was as frothy as *2001*.'

Perhaps if less than $27 million had been spent on *One From The Heart* the reviews might have been more favourable. Yet, almost the only thing going for the film is precisely the amount spent on the dazzling sets and technology. The plot, as in most musicals, was slender and functional.

Hank (Frederic Forrest) and Frannie (Teri Garr) have been living together in a modest home in Las Vegas for five years. On their anniversary, the Fourth of July, each brings home a gift for the other, revealing their contrasting ambitions. Hank has spent his savings on the deed of their home, and Frannie has bought air tickets for Bora Bora. After an argument, they pair off with others, Frannie with suave Latino Ray (Raul Julia), and Hank with Leila (Nastassia Kinski), a circus acrobat, during one night in Las Vegas, before they are reunited.

'Filmed entirely on the stages of Zoetrope studios' boasted the end credit. Yet, even taking into account the fact that audiences of the 1980s found it difficult to respond to studio-bound films any longer, it might have worked if there had been a better screenplay, dancing, songs and lyrics, and more genuine feeling. What was lacking in *One From The Heart* was heart. Coppola himself admitted that it failed to engage as a love story, and ended up more about 'the look and technology.' It is possible that the alienating quality of the film came from the manner in which Coppola made it, cutting himself off from the actors and crew by playing Big Brother from his trailer.

One From The Heart returned less than $2 million at the box office. Both audiences and investors were tiring of Coppola's artistic and financial vicissitudes, and Zoetrope was put up for sale. Coppola was offered $20 million, two million less than the final budget of *One From The Heart*. But Jack Singer, who had already served Zoetrope with a foreclosure notice, rejected the bid. Meanwhile, Francis decided that the only course of action was to escape into adolescence.

12 Teen Dreams

Rumble Fish will be to *The Outsiders* what *Apocalypse Now* was to *The Godfather*. You could say it's an art film for kids. You could say it's kind of an existentialist beatnik movie.

In March 1980, Coppola received a letter from Jo Ellen Misakian, the librarian at Lone Star School, Fresno County, written 'on behalf of the students and faculty.' Because they had adored *The Black Stallion*, which had been released the year before, they felt that Zoetrope should now film S. E. Hinton's *The Outsiders*, a teenage novel about the rivalry between two groups of kids in 1960s Oklahoma, the lower-class 'Greasers' and the upper-crust 'Socs'. 'We have a student body of 324. I feel our students are representative of the youth of America. Everyone who has read the book, regardless of ethnic or economic background, has enthusiastically endorsed this project.'

Coppola read the book, and thought it would make a good movie. Susie Hinton had written *The Outsiders*, her first novel, when she was fifteen. Now thirty, she was the wife of a Texas shoe salesman and the author of three more books for teenagers, *Tex*, *That Was Then, This Is Now*, and *Rumble Fish*. Zoetrope was so broke that they could only offer her a paltry five hundred dollars with a percentage of the profits and a part in the movie. To Coppola's surprise and delight, Hinton accepted.

Although Coppola planned to shoot the film on location in a naturalistic style – no expensive sets – without expensive stars, he still had to raise around $10 million from other sources. Despite the disastrous losses on *One From The Heart*, he managed to do this on the strength of Warner Bros.' agreement to distribute the film.

The cast of virtual unknowns that Coppola gathered for *The Outsiders* now reads like Who's Who of the Brat Pack, the hottest young stars of the 1980s. In the lead of the shy and sensitive Ponyboy was sixteen-year-old C. Thomas Howell, a former junior rodeo circuit champion, who had had a bit part in *E.T.* With him were Matt Dillon, two years older, who had just completed *Tex*, the first Hinton book to be filmed, and seventeen-

year-old Diane Lane, already a veteran of six pictures. Others included
Tom Cruise (yet to get his front teeth straightened), Emilio Estevez, the
eldest son of Martin Sheen, using his father's original surname, Rob
Lowe (in his screen debut), Ralph Macchio, a year before becoming *The
Karate Kid*, and Patrick Swayze, at thirty, the only one of the leading
performers beyond his teens.

In March 1982, Coppola and his crew flew to Tulsa. There, he converted
an abandoned schoolhouse into a computerized studio where he videotaped rehearsals in what had been the gym. Although he had brought all
his electronics and his silver trailer, this time he was on the set all the
time with the actors. Wearing a French beret and corduroys, Coppola got
on very well with the kids, and they responded well to him, Matt Dillon
dubbing him 'Father Film'. However, in order to create tension between
the gangs, Coppola gave the 'Socs' better off-screen accommodation,
food and treatment, while the 'Greasers' were provided with poorer facilities. But he allowed all of them a beer after each day's long shoot.
   As usual there was some further Coppola family representation on the
movie. His elder son, Gio, then seventeen, had worked as an assistant on
One From The Heart, and Italia and Carmine had appeared in a brief
scene in the elevator in the same movie. This time, both Gio and Roman
acted as associate producers, and twelve-year-old Sofia (under the pseu-
donym of Domino) had a small part as an annoying little girl. For the film,
Francis asked his father to compose 'schmaltzy classical music.'

While on location, Coppola read Hinton's third novel *Rumble Fish*. He
decided to prolong his stay and film it back to back with *The Outsiders*,
the same technicians and with Matt Dillon and Diane Lane starring.
Supporting them were twenty-seven-year-old Mickey Rourke as
Motorcycle Boy, Dillon's big brother, and two survivors from *Apocalypse
Now*, Dennis Hopper and Larry Fishburne. Aside from bit parts for Sofia
(aka Domino) and Gio, Nicholas Coppola, Francis' nephew was seventh-
billed. 'In my Uncle Francis' imagination my role was very much like my
father [August], so that he had me sort of looking like him and that was
uncomfortable. I was terrified, but at that time I didn't know how to say
no. He wouldn't let me create my own thoughts for the character, so that
was when I decided to change my name.' *Rumble Fish* was the only film
which featured Nicholas Coppola before he emerged as Nicolas Cage,
who was to make two further films for his uncle.
   For *Rumble Fish*, Coppola decided to compose the music himself,
using mainly percussion. To help him with the score, he got Stewart
Copeland, the American drummer with the English band The Police,
to improvise a rhythm track. Francis soon realized that Copeland was

a far better musician than he, and let him take over. Coppola also hired Michael Smuin, a choreographer with the San Francisco Ballet, to stage the fight scene, and a street dance for Diana Scarwid and Mickey Rourke.

Coppola imagined *The Outsiders* as a *Gone With The Wind* for kids (whereas *Rumble Fish* was 'an art film for kids'), not so much in content but in style: the film's title moves across the screen in the same manner, one of the boys is reading the novel, and there are several glowing (relevant) sunsets and sunrises with the characters silhouetted against them. Gold, as mentioned in the Robert Frost poem, 'Nothing Gold Can Stay', which one of the boys reads, comes to represent youthful idealism. In other words, Coppola attempted, unashamedly, to recreate the world of early Technicolored romantic melodramas, as well as 1950s juvenile deliquent movies such as *Rebel Without A Cause*.

The story revolves around two 'Greasers', Ponyboy (C. Thomas Howell) and Johnny (Ralph Macchio) who get into a fight with some 'Socs' because they have a friendship with Cherry Valance (Diane Lane), a Soc girl. Defending his friend, Johnny fatally stabs one of their rivals. Dallas (Matt Dillon) helps them to hide out in an abandoned church. When a group of children visit the church and get caught in a fire, Johnny is critically injured while going to their rescue, his final words being, 'Stay gold, stay gold.' 'That's what you get for helping people,' the outwardly cynical, but soft-hearted, Dallas concludes.

With hardly an adult in sight, Coppola wholeheartedly enters the world of semi-tough youths, rapturously concentrating on the pubescent faces of the up-and-coming stars. It is also filled with the nostalgia for Coppola's own youth when he was a member of a street gang called the Bay Rats, and saw films like *Beach Blanket Bingo*, which the kids in *The Outsiders* watch at a drive-in. On the other hand, the idealistic tone is counterbalanced by the story of revenge, which leads to a vividly realized rumble in the rain and mud, and violent death.

The T-shirted Matt Dillon, so good in *The Outsiders*, is used to even greater effect in *Rumble Fish*, a darker side of the previous, more idealistic, film. As Rusty-James, he is a none-too-bright layabout, with an alcoholic father (Dennis Hopper). His older brother, The Motorcycle Boy (Mickey Rourke), whom he idolizes, returns from California in the midst of a knife fight in which Rusty-James is wounded. Towards the end, after The Motorcycle Boy releases birds from a pet shop, and the fish into the river, he is shot down by a cop (William Smith) who bears a grudge against him. As he lies martyred, Rusty-James faces the sea, like the boy at the end of François Truffaut's *The 400 Blows*.

Future stars (left to right): Emilio Estevez, Rob Lowe, C. Thomas Howell, Matt Dillon, Ralph Macchio, Patrick Swayze and Tom Cruise in a publicity still for The Outsiders **(1983).**

However, *Rumble Fish*, with its expressionistic camera angles, shadowy lighting, and atmospheric nether-world locations, is closer to the aesthetic world of Orson Welles, particularly *Touch of Evil*. It was shot superbly in black and white, with time-lapse photography and intermittent colour, that of the Red and Blue fish of the title so loved by The Motorcycle Boy, the only colour in his life. Both films proved that Coppola was not content to make genre movies in a conventional way, but to experiment with form, making them two of his best and most personal films.

By September 1982, shooting on both films was complete, on schedule and on budget. However, Warners, who were lukewarm about the rough cut of *The Outsiders*, were not interested in distributing a second teen picture, and Coppola had desperately to find another distributor quickly. Luckily, Universal agreed to take *Rumble Fish* as a two-picture deal with Abel Gance's 1927 masterpiece *Napoléon*, the rights of which Zoetrope had obtained in 1979.

Soon after, while Coppola was reluctantly cutting half an hour from the 120-minute running time of *The Outsiders* at Warners' insistence, bankers were warning him that they would have to foreclose unless he came up with $7 million in three months, before 14 January 1983. Despite being unable to meet the deadline, rescue operations continued to keep Zoetrope afloat for a further year.

Residual income from *Apocalypse Now*, and healthy box-office receipts for *The Outsiders*, brought something into the Zoetrope coffers. Coppola also had hopes for his next project, little realizing that it would be another heart-breaking saga of wasted money and opportunities.

13 Black Days and White Nights

The Cotton Club is a personal movie even though I was the hireling. Its message is that talent is the only thing that can break servitude.

In February 1983, Coppola received a call from Robert Evans, now an independent producer, who asked him if he could help on the script of a film about Harlem's legendary Cotton Club. He had commissioned Mario Puzo to write it, but millionaire arms dealer Adnan Khashoggi, who had invested $2 million in the film, didn't like Puzo's screenplay. Evans sent it to Coppola, who read it and thought it useless. He agreed to rewrite it for $500,000, which Evans paid gladly. But when the first draft was delivered, none of the investors liked it. Their main criticism was that the star part, for which Richard Gere was being paid $1.5 million, plus ten per cent of the gross, had been diminished.

In order to salvage what Coppola saw as a picture about black people that they could be proud of, he invited Gere, and two black performers, Gregory Hines and Marilyn Matthews, to his Napa Valley estate where they spent ten days trying to write a more coherent script that would both please black audiences and reinstate the importance of Gere's role.

Then Coppola began to imagine how he would direct it. He saw The Cotton Club, where the audience was exclusively white and the performers exclusively black, as a microcosm of an era. 'I, being a hired hand, was probably attracted to a scenario that sees all its characters as hired hands of one sort or another,' he recalled. He then offered to direct the picture for a fee of $2.5 million, outright control of the production to final cut and approval of the release prints. In June 1983, Evans accepted these terms, and agreed to give Coppola a slice of the gross profits.

To get the period accuracy he wanted, Coppola engaged William Kennedy, the author of a trilogy of novels on the Prohibition era, to help him on the screenplay. In a month, Coppola and Kennedy produced twelve different complete versions. They finally made a decision on which version to use, and sent it to the printer a few weeks before shooting was to begin.

Richard Gere and Diane Lane in The Cotton Club **(1984).**

Pre-production had been in full swing for six months before Coppola took over all aspects of it. Wanting his own people around him, he sacked many of the crew already under contract, including cinematographer John Alonzo and music director Jerry Wexler, at the cost of large settlements.

Most of the rehearsals (as would the shoot) took place at the Kaufman Astoria Studios in New York, where the director encouraged the cast to improvise while he recorded them on video. Then he would incorporate the best of their improvisations into the ever-changing script. This method suited some of the cast, but Richard Gere objected forcefully. When shooting began on 22 August 1983 – there was still no final script – Gere didn't show up. He had disappeared, only to turn up a week later. It seems that the star had been worried that he might never see any money, and wanted his huge fee up front. Evans gave in to the star's wishes, as well as agreeing to pay him an extra $250,000 for every day the film ran over schedule.

Things went well for the first few weeks, although Coppola was under pressure from the Doumani brothers, Las Vegas nightclub owners, who were prime investors in the film, to cut costs of the shoot which was running at $1.2 million a week. Tensions began to mount on the set, bringing clashes between Coppola and Gere. On one occasion, Coppola yelled at Gere, 'Listen to me, you don't like me, you never liked me at all. But let me tell you something, I'm not only older than you, I'm richer than you. Now get out of here!'

In September, Coppola fired the choreographer Dyson Lowell, who was also an executive producer, and seventeen technicians, some of whom had apparently complained about Coppola's nepotism – son Gio was second-unit director and montage editor, daughter Sofia played the street kid who gets killed, nephew Nicolas Cage had the part of 'Mad Dog' Dwyer, Gere's hoodlum kid brother, and Cage's brother Marc had a bit part.

Because of continued pressure from the Doumani brothers, many of the big dance numbers had to be rushed. In addition, Coppola had not been paid his salary. 'Who needs this,' he stormed at Evans. 'It's not my picture. You need me. I don't need you.' At one stage, Coppola even banned Evans from the set. Robert Osborne, a journalist who watched some of the making of the film, wrote: 'Waste of time, waste of shots, waste of money. Over a million dollars, for example, was spent just on extras for a single nightclub sequence because of insufficient preparations . . . . Other accusations include nepotism, also drugs. One cast member told me, "There was so much coke on the set you couldn't believe it."'

Bob Hoskins, who played the owner of the club, recalled: 'I gained twenty pounds waiting around for something to happen. You sort of sit around and eat and drink and philosophize, and suddenly you've forgotten what you do for a living . . . . Francis would just toss things out in the air. I could never figure Francis out at all. I just did what he told me. It's into Aladdin's cave with him.'

It is always surprising, after the horror stories on the making of a number of Coppola's movies, that they should turn out to be so splendid, and *The Cotton Club* is no exception. The style and plot make a pointed allusion to the Warner Bros. gangster movies of the 1930s, starring James Cagney (one of the many stars who 'appear' at the Harlem Nightclub in the movie), Edward G. Robinson, and George Raft whose persona influenced the Gere character of Dixie Dwyer, who makes a film in Hollywood called *Mob Boss*.

While the film is never a direct pastiche, Coppola nevertheless plays brilliantly with the conventions of the early gangster picture, even down to the spectacular montage sequences (directed by Gian-Carlo Coppola), like those by Stefan Vorkapich in the 1930s. The consciously arch 'happy ending', has most of the surviving characters doing a dance number in Grand Central Station. In addition to these elements, Coppola explores the theme of racial prejudice, both among the 'wop', 'kike' and 'spick' mobsters, and between the management of the club and the 'niggers'.

Dixie starts off as a cornet player (Gere did his own playing), but when he accidentally saves the life of Dutch Schultz (James Remar, reminiscent of Paul Muni in *Scarface*), he finds himself working for the thankful racketeer. One of his duties is to look after Dutch's young moll, Vera Cicero (Diane Lane), with whom he falls in love. Just as he is getting deeper and deeper into the dangerous world of bootleggers, he escapes to Hollywood. After Schultz is killed at the instigation of Owney Madden (Bob Hoskins) and Frenchy Demange (Fred Gwynne), owners of the Cotton Club, Dixie and Vera are able to get together.

The whole story revolves around the Cotton Club, at which exclusively black entertainers perform for exclusively white audiences, so that the action is punctuated with dozens of song and dance routines, mainly executed by Gregory and Maurice Hines, Lonette McKee and a terrific troupe of chorus boys and girls. One of the few reproaches that could be levelled at Coppola is the way in which he cuts away from most of the numbers, either to the audience or a concurrent scene, not allowing them to develop or terminate naturally. As in *Finian's Rainbow*, a simpler approach might have been more effective. However, this technique is justified towards the end, when Coppola rapidly cuts between Gregory Hines' rapid-fire tapping and the slaughter of Schultz, a *tour de force* of editing, both sound and visual.

The picture is rich in other inventive moments, such as blood dripping onto Vera from a chandelier after a gangster has been violently

killed; light casting shadows of net curtains on the faces of a couple
making love . . . . There are also poignantly human scenes, such as a
session in the Hoofers' Club, where old-time tap dancers get together to
demonstrate their routines, and the love-hate interplay between Bob
Hoskins and Fred Gwynne when the latter returns after being kidnapped,
complaining of the derisory sum Hoskins offered for him.

The dialogue is consistently sharp and witty, and the costumes and
decor, eye-catching as they are, never overwhelm the foreground as the
sets in *One From The Heart* were inclined to do Apart from Richard
Gere's rather too brilliantined charm, the well-chosen cast is impecca-
ble, all seeming aptly period, with 'appearances' by lookalikes of Duke
Ellington, Gloria Swanson, Charlie Chaplin and a hallucinatory recre-
ation by Larry Marshall of Cab Calloway singing 'Minnie the Moocher'.

After *The Cotton Club* was finally completed in December 1983, it was
followed by the raucous sound of suing and countersuing by almost all
the leading financial participants. Against this background of legal wran-
gles, the film opened to mixed reviews and a reasonable box-office
success, though not enough to meet the debts.

In February 1984, Zoetrope Studios in Los Angeles was sold to Jack
Singer, the Canadian financier, for $12.3 million. However, as Coppola
pointed out, 'It's important to remember that Zoetrope Company [San
Francisco], as opposed to Zoetrope Studios, has been alive for thirteen
years now, and if we sell the studio it has nothing to do with our company
and all its assets.' He would now have to take on almost any paid project,
though with stories about his extravagance and megalomania on *The
Cotton Club* still resounding through the film industry, offers did not
exactly flood in.

14 Forward to the Past

Movies make more money than you think. All my projects kept kicking in dough, and the creditors saw it and let me stay out of bankruptcy.

Despite the crushing financial pressures upon him, and another expensive failure hanging around his neck, Coppola continued to instigate projects for the now slimmed-down Zoetrope Company. But, at forty-five, the overweight director was beginning to question his vocation.

I'm not sure I have a career any more [he told a journalist towards the end of 1984]. I'm an oddball in the eyes of the public. I'm beginning to be more and more estranged from the movie industry . . . . People have been frightened by what they read about me. I've had a rough time for the past few years. I had my fun and now I'm paying for it. But why was it so bad that I wanted a little studio to turn out movies? . . . I still love to make movies although I find the system a little trying. On the big films, you don't really get your hands on the money. It gets moved around in lawyers' offices.

Coppola found some sanctuary on his Napa Valley estate, where he involved himself in winemaking. Notwithstanding his huge debts, he hired a great French oenologist, André Tchelistcheff, as winemaking consultant. Coppola had acquired further vineyards in the neighbourhood, and developed his own wine called Niebaum-Coppola Rubicon, 'a claret blend of Cabernet Sauvignon, Cabernet Franc and Merlot', which was sold at around thirty-five dollars a bottle in the early 1980s. He donated twenty per cent of the profits to AIDS causes and various children's charities. In general, the wine was well-received in the press, the 1979 Rubicon being described by wine expert Robert N. Parker as 'a rich bouquet of tarry, black cherry fruit and oak. It is very concentrated, full-bodied and, while drinkable now, will keep eight to ten years.' However, another writer thought Coppola's wines were like his films: 'They're expensive, take a long time to produce, and sit around for years before being released.'

In 1985, Coppola was commissioned to make *Rip Van Winkle* for the Home
Box Office 'Faerie Tale Theater' television series. Coppola admired Eiko
Ishioka, the Japanese designer responsible for the striking sets for Paul
Schrader's *Mishima*, on which he had been executive producer, and asked
her to help him with the fifty-minute TV movie, which he shot in five days
at a Los Angeles studio. For the Washington Irving classic tale, she created
a 'human mountain', derived from the Kabuki theatre, which consisted of
a few people moving under a sheet of canvas that changes shape and
colour to suit the mood of the scene. (Ishioka would make an even greater
impression seven years later with *Bram Stoker's Dracula*.) Coppola also
used a new computerized matting technique called Ultimatte. This
enabled him to combine several moving mattes to create multiple superimpositions. 'I don't want to be limited by reality any more,' he declared.
Again, on *Rip Van Winkle*, he surrounded himself with a cast of intimates:
Harry Dean Stanton, who had been in *The Godfather Part II* and *One From
The Heart*, played the title role; Coppola's sister Talia Shire was Rip's
nagging wife, and Sofia Coppola his daughter. He also had the smallest
budget since his early nudie pictures. 'The bigger the budget, the less
freedom you have and the less money,' he claimed.

Ironically, Coppola's next film had a budget of over $20 million, and was
only fifteen minutes long, making *Captain Eo*, starring Michael Jackson,
the most expensive short in screen history. Walt Disney Productions,
which had a contract with Jackson, who wrote the songs, co-funded the
production with Eastman Kodak who wanted to show off its new 70mm 3-D
process. George Lucas, who was executive producer, brought in Coppola,
Vittorio Storaro and Walter Murch. As most of the film, shot in the Laird
Studios in LA, would consist of special effects created by Disney technicians, Coppola's job of directing the mere actors was soon over. Michael
Jackson played a space marshal battling the forces of a She-Devil Supreme
(Anjelica Huston) on a colourless planet beyond the solar system. With the
help of music, dance and lasers, Eo and his warriors convert this mono-
chrome regime into a playground of joy and colour. *Captain Eo*, viewed
through so-called '3-U' glasses, and with a quintuphonic soundtrack, was
shown exclusively in seven hundred-seat theatres in Disneyland
(California) and Disney World (Florida) from September 1985.

About a year previously, Ray Stark, producer and president of Rastar,
had contacted Coppola to direct *Peggy Sue Got Married*, the title of which
was taken from a Buddy Holly song. Stark, for whom Coppola had written the unused screenplay of *Reflections in a Golden Eye* back in 1967,
explained that he was third choice, both Jonathan Demme and Penny
Marshall having left the project. Debra Winger, who was to play the title

role, was hospitalized with a severe back ailment, and Kathleen Turner, who took over, first had to finish *The Jewel of the Nile* in Morocco.

So it was not until August 1985 that Coppola began to shoot *Peggy Sue Got Married*, his first film since *The Rain People* in which a woman had the leading role. Kathleen Turner had emerged as one of the boldest and classiest of screen goddesses of the 1980s, especially in Lawrence Kasdan's *Body Heat* (1981) and John Huston's *Prizzi's Honor* (1985). Keeping the family contact, Coppola cast his twenty-one-year-old nephew Nicolas Cage, now a rising star since *Moonstruck* and *Birdie* the previous year, as her nerdy, nasal husband, with daughter Sofia Coppola (billed under her real name) as Peggy Sue's brat of a little sister.

As a stand-in for the small mid-western town in the film, the small town of Pentaluna, California was found: an ideal location because it had all the elements necessary for the plot and was less than an hour's drive from the Coppolas' Napa Valley vineyard.

After he had videotaped the rehearsals, as had become his custom, Coppola began the shoot which lasted about eight weeks. The cinematographer Jordan Cronenweth, with whom the director had never worked but whose camera work he had admired in *Blade Runner*, was asked to infuse the film with rich, saturated colours, while production designer Dean Tavoularis sprayed the sidewalks with yellow paint to give them a nostalgic glow. In fact, the recapturing of the dreamy essence of 1960 to which the heroine returns from twenty-five years in the future is the film's most effective component. Filming proceeded relatively smoothly, but when Coppola looked at the final cut, he disliked it intensely, especially the final scene.

Keen to finish on time and on budget, he had filmed the scene from 1 a.m. to 4 p.m. on the last day of the scheduled shooting. He felt that the fatigue of the cast came through, and that the scene was too sweet when he wanted it bittersweet. He therefore asked Tri-Star if he could retake it. As he had brought the movie in under budget, they agreed. It took a few days to re-shoot the sequence, in which Turner is seen looking at her reflection in the mirror, a 'reflection' of the opening shot.

Of *Peggy Sue Got Married*, Ray Stark commented, 'I felt this film was the chance for Francis to make a small, intimate film with a simple story, and the critics would say "Hey, Francis, it's good, you made a nice little simple story. It's not a brilliant Francis Coppola film", and frankly it isn't, and anyone who says it is, is crazy.'

Peggy Sue Bodell, who has just separated from her philandering husband Charlie (Nicolas Cage), is dressing for her twenty-fifth High School reunion. Attending the reunion with her teenage daughter (Helen Hunt), Peggy Sue is crowned class queen, but seeing Charlie enter the

Kathleen Turner (left) in the title role of Peggy Sue Got Married
(1986), with Joan Allen (centre) and Catherine Hicks.

room, she faints. When she awakens, she finds herself back in 1960, a seventeen-year-old high school senior, but with her forty-two-year-old mind intact. (She appears a teenager to the other characters, but the same adult to the audience.) Although she has a chance to make a match with a handsome beatnik (Kevin O'Connor) and an intellectual (Barry Miller), she is trapped into marrying Charlie by getting pregnant by him. Then she wakes up in a hospital bed in the 1980s, with a repentant Charlie at her side. As in *The Rain People* and *One From The Heart*, the woman gives up freedom to return to her husband in the end.

Because the vastly successful *Back To The Future* had appeared the year before, people considered that *Peggy Sue Got Married* was cashing in on it, although the superior and deeper later film was in development long before. Both films share the pleasure derived from the situation of characters living in the past, who have a superior knowledge of the future. Although *Peggy Sue* has the less interesting, indeed somewhat perfunctory, device for time travelling, it has the more interesting premise viz questioning whether if one had the chance to go back in time, would one make the same mistakes. There is genuine emotion in the scenes where Peggy Sue meets her parents, whom she realizes she had taken for granted, and her long-dead grandparents.

Thirty-one-year-old Kathleen Turner, who was Oscar-nominated for her role, pulls off the difficult feat of playing a seventeen-year-old with a forty-two-year-old mind and body (unlike Robin Williams in *Jack*, who has the mind of a ten-year-old in a forty-year-old body), managing, with almost no make-up, to suggest the adolescent in gestures and speech.

Nicolas Cage, on the other hand, seems to have had little direction from his uncle, and it is hard to accept him as an older man (with unconvincing make-up), or that this obnoxious character could ever have held any attraction for Peggy Sue.

Peggy Sue Got Married had its premiere at the closing night of the New York Film Festival on 5 October 1986. Ironically, the one film in which Coppola did not feel much involvement or personal commitment – he even had little hand in the screenplay – turned out to be his biggest hit of the 1980s, and garnered reasonably good reviews. Kathleen Turner, cinematographer Jordan Cronenweth, and costume designer Theodora Van Runkle were all nominated for Oscars, and Cronenweth was given the first annual award by the American Society of Cinematographers for his work on the film. *Peggy Sue Got Married*, plus the receipts from *The Outsiders* and *The Cotton Club*, managed to go a long way towards paying off some of Coppola's enormous debts, but this was not able to assuage the pain of a very personal tragedy.

15 Burying the Future

> I've always had the feeling that whatever movie I worked on, my own life would be part of it, like a twilight zone. So many things that happened on *Apocalypse* reflected the story and the characters, and then to do a movie about the burying of young boys . . . and then to find out that my own young boy would die right in the midst of it . . . .'

In the spring of 1985, Coppola received a lunch invitation from Victor Kaufman, boss of Tri-Star Pictures. He suggested Coppola direct a screen version of *Gardens of Stone*, the 1983 novel by Nicholas Proffitt about the Old Guard, the army unit in charge of funerals at Arlington National Cemetery in Washington. Although Ronald Bass had already written the screenplay, Coppola would still be able to co-produce and choose the people with whom he wanted to work.

First, permission had to be obtained from the army to film at Arlington. Luckily, when a high-ranking general was told that Coppola had written the screenplay of *Patton*, his favourite movie, he offered the army's full co-operation. This meant allowing access to Arlington, Fort Myer and Fort Belvoir, providing helicopters, six hundred extras, uniforms and equipment, military training, technical advice and haircuts for the actors playing soldiers. Unlike *Apocalypse Now*, *Gardens of Stone* would show the military in a flattering light, though the brass objected to two scenes in the script, which Coppola dutifully excised: a young widow spitting on her husband's grave at Arlington, shouting, 'At least now I know where you're spending your nights'; and an angry sergeant punching an enlisted man. The film was dedicated to the 3rd Infantry, the Old Guard of the Army.

The cast was headed by James Caan, who was making a comeback after five years away from the screen because of 'substance abuse'. Although he had received professional help and got himself cured, nobody would employ him in Hollywood and he was deeply indebted to Coppola for giving him a fresh start. Finding a new gravitas, Caan was utterly convincing as the stiff-necked, but tender-hearted Sergeant Hazard. Others with whom Coppola had previously worked were Anjelica Huston (*Captain Eo*) and Larry Fishburne (*Apocalypse Now*, *Rumble Fish*, *The Cotton Club*), Sam Bottoms (*Apocalypse Now*), Lonette McKee (*The Cotton Club*), the cinematographer Jordan Cronenweth (*Peggy Sue Got Married*), Dean Tavoularis, his usual production designer, and Carmine Coppola, who hadn't composed a score for his son's films since *The Outsiders*. Twenty-two-year-old Gio (Gian-Carlo) was second-unit director.

The whole family had moved to Virginia to be near the locations. Dean Tavoularis had found buildings in the Greek and Roman style, which were used 'to give the film an eternal look and feel. The architecture helps complement the story which, itself, is timeless.'

During the two weeks of rehearsals, which Coppola videotaped, the cast, including James Caan and James Earl Jones as army officers, spent hours drilling, perfecting their military bearing and learning to use sabres and rifles. For safety reasons, the army asked that the helicopters be shot in natural light, with no exterior lighting, something that would make them difficult to see. This was solved by Cronenweth and Coppola by shooting the helicopters at sunset, which made them stand out against the sky.

Gardens of Stone is set at Fort Myer, a peaceful barracks near Washington. The time is 1968, and the Vietnam war is still raging. The film begins with a military funeral at Arlington, and then goes into an extended flashback which covers the events leading up to the funeral. Sergeant Hazard (James Caan) is a cultured and compassionate soldier who feels that there is 'nothing to win, and no way of winning it' in Vietnam. He trains the young recruits – 'toy soldiers' as he calls them – for the Old Guard, but he would rather use his combat experience to train them for battle. Despite their differing views, he has an affair with Samantha (Anjelica Huston, showing more warmth than in previous roles), an anti-war reporter on the *Washington Post*. Sergeant Hazard has also found a surrogate son among the recruits, a Lieutenant Willow (D. B. Sweeney), who is the son of a friend with whom he had been in Korea. The young man volunteers for Vietnam, where he is soon killed. It is to Lieutenant Willow's funeral that the film returns at the end.

Not long after shooting had commenced, on Monday, 26 May, Gio, his girlfriend Jacqueline de la Fontaine, and Griffin O'Neal, the unruly twenty-one-year-old son of the actor Ryan O'Neal, had lunch, with a bottle of wine to celebrate the fact that Gio had just landed the job of second-unit director on a Whoopie Goldberg picture, *Jumpin' Jack Flash*. Lunch over, Gio and Griffin bought a six-pack and hired a four-teen-foot McKee speedboat, which they took out on the South River near Annapolis, leaving Jacqueline ashore after a preliminary ride. Around

5.15 p.m., O'Neal took the boat on a fast bouncing course between two larger boats. There was plenty of room to get through, but he didn't notice that there was a taut tow-line linking the two boats. As the craft struck the rope, Gio was jerked off his feet, his head striking the deck. Somehow O'Neal got the boat back to shore, where Gio was rushed to the Anne Arundel County General Hospital. He had sustained terrible head injuries, and was pronounced dead on arrival. O'Neal, who had previous drug and driving convictions, was found guilty of 'reckless endangerment', fined two hundred dollars, and given eighteen months probation. At the hearing, Jacqueline, who was three-months pregnant by Gio, described how O'Neal 'was driving really crazy . . . . He was going wild.'

Since the age of sixteen, Gio had worked closely with his father, who idolized him. There was never any resentment among Francis' associates towards 'the Coppola kid', who was both well-mannered and very professional. Naturally, Coppola was devastated by his son's death, and for more than a year he could not bring himself to talk about it. Nevertheless, he decided to press on with the shooting of *Gardens of Stone*, and was on the set a few hours after the death. It was the only way he could keep his sanity. 'Work has that quality of being something you can do, as opposed to sitting around and weeping,' he said in 1987. Yet there was a lot of weeping among the crew, much of it brought on by the sombre nature of the film which contained funerals of young men, at which many of the tears of the cast were genuine. Coppola drove himself relentlessly to finish on schedule, which he did. On 5 August 1986, the last principal photography of *Gardens of Stone* was completed. It had taken just eight weeks and was only seven per cent over budget.

The shadow of Gio's death lingers over *Gardens of Stone*. It has a mellow, autumnal tone, both in the hue of the photography, and in the playing and script. Coppola treats the subject soberly – there is no rapid cutting, clever dissolves or dramatic camera angles, only the interpolation of actual footage from the Vietnam war, which is constantly pouring from television sets and dominates everyone's lives. Unusually for a Coppola picture, there were no spectacular set-pieces, and the little action was confined to war games, a sort of 'junior prom' *Apocalypse Now*. The military rituals are lovingly observed, and the characters never patronized. Here, as in many of his films that echo others of the past, Coppola seems to see a cliché coming and then dodges it just in time.

With its focus on a small community in a fort, surrounded by hostile forces, *Gardens of Stone* resembles John Ford's cavalry films. But, most of all, it is almost an updated remake of *The Long Gray Line*, Ford's sentimental study of West Point Academy. Like Ford, Coppola concentrates on

James Caan happy to be making a comeback in Gardens of
Stone **(1987).**

the superb actors and the interaction between them, especially the three
differing and tender relationships that James Caan has with Anjelica
Huston (romantic), James Earl Jones (fraternal), and D. B. Sweeney
(paternal).

When *Gardens of Stone* was released in May 1987, most critics, inexplicably, were left cold and didn't spare Coppola's feelings. It was generally greeted in a lukewarm manner, and failed at the box office. By that
time, however, Coppola had moved on to a project far closer to his heart.

16 The Dream Factory

Before World War II, the United States had a spirit of inventiveness. Our heroes were people who took great ideas and made them into the industries of the future. But after the war came the marketing era, the Harvard Business School philosophy of managing companies, and I believe that the creative person . . . was suppressed. *Tucker* is this story. America needs people like Tucker if it is to regain the shine it had in the past.

Tucker: The Man and his Dream had germinated in Coppola's mind for more than a decade, though the idea could be said to date from his childhood. In the mid-1940s, Carmine invested five thousand dollars, a large proportion of his savings, in the company which produced an innovative automobile designed by Preston Tucker. Francis recalled being taken by his father to a car show to see the prototype. 'I thought it was really beautiful. I remember the day. I remember the buttons on the car. And I kept asking my father when my Tucker was going to come. And then he told me, little by little, that it was never going to come because all the other auto companies thought it was too good and they put him out of business.' Since then Preston Tucker, with whom he identified, became a hero to Francis.

In 1976, Coppola announced that a film about Preston Tucker was in pre-production, with the possibility that Marlon Brando would play the inventor. Then Coppola saw it as 'a sort of Brechtian musical in which Tucker would be the main story, but it would also involve Edison and Henry Ford and Firestone and Carnegie.' Leonard Bernstein would compose the music, Betty Comden and Adolf Green would write the lyrics and Jack Nicholson would star. So serious was Coppola about this conception that Bernstein spent two weeks at the Napa estate to discuss the musical, but it was abandoned as impractical. There is still, however, something of the musical in the way some of the set-pieces are staged.

Ten years later, the project resurfaced, but this time as a straight biopic. George Lucas, who had established Lucasfilm Ltd with the profits from *Star Wars*, offered to finance the picture, and put his studio's

Coppola cutting Tucker: The Man and His Dream **(1988),
overseen by George Lucas (left), executive producer.**

advanced technology at Coppola's disposal. Although Lucas had just had two expensive flops, *Howard the Duck* and *Labyrinth*, he accepted that *Tucker* would need a budget of $25 million. He did insist, however, with the horror stories of *Apocalypse Now* and *The Cotton Club* still fresh, that a complete, coherent screenplay be written before the shoot began. Given Coppola's screenwriting talents and that the subject meant a great deal to him personally, it is ironic that he did not write his own script.

With a screenplay by Arnold Shulman and David Seidler, *Tucker: The Man and his Dream* began shooting 13 April 1987. Much of it was filmed on location in and around the Bay Area of San Francisco. A Victorian manor in Sonoma stood in for the Tucker home in Michigan, while many of the sets were built inside the giant Deco-style Model A Ford factory on the waterfront in Richmond, California. Twenty-two of the forty-six surviving Tucker cars were found (only fifty were ever built), though two additional models had to be constructed in fibreglass for scenes that might have damaged a real car. Coppola's own dark red Tucker with the number plate GIO 2 28 was used as the prototype.

For once there were no Coppolas in the film, although Carmine wrote some incidental music – the main score was by British pop singer Joe Jackson. Vittorio Storaro was the cinematographer, and he and Coppola agreed to shoot *Tucker* in the sort of unsaturated colours that would be reminiscent of the *Life* magazine features of the 1940s.

In order to bring off the complex movements of the camera he required, Coppola, unlike his earlier ideas about allowing actors liberty of movement, instructed them to hit their marks with exactitude. Jeff Bridges, who was playing the title role, complained that it was 'like acting in a Rembrandt painting. I've never done a film this complicated as far as camera moves and lights are concerned. To act in it almost requires a different technique.' Bridges got round the problem by moving like a robot through the first take, making sure to hit his marks, and supplying the emotion from the second take.

During the shoot, Coppola used the sort of trick he had often pulled to get more realistic performances from his cast (such as giving the boys playing the Socs superior accommodation to the Greasers on *The Outsiders*). For the sequence when the first Tucker Tornando is launched, he called the group of extras hours before the shoot, getting them to sit on hard seats under one hundred and ninety-two light bulbs so that, while the lengthy delays take place before the car is wheeled on, the crowd grows genuinely angry.

Because a Director's Guild strike was imminent during the summer, Coppola and his crew worked fast and hard enough to end principal photography by 17 July, ahead of schedule. It is easily forgotten, because of the infamous stories surrounding *Apocalypse Now* and, to a lesser degree, *The Cotton Club*, Coppola generally, from his earliest days with Corman, shot quickly and economically.

Tucker: The Man and his Dream plunges straight into its subject, unlike the usual biopics that detail the childhood, adolescence and love life of the subject. Preston Tucker (Jeff Bridges) is already a man in his thirties, married to a supportive wife (Joan Allen), and the father of four children. He has designed the prototype for the *Tucker* Tornado, but needs finance to build one. For this purpose, he hires Abe Karatz (Martin Landau) as his financial advisor. Unfortunately, he is blocked by The Big Three automobile manufacturers, who are represented by a Detroit senator (a tasty uncredited cameo by Lloyd Bridges, Jeff's father), and he loses overall control of the company to Bennington (Dean Goodman), the Chairman of the Board. Tucker later has to appear before a grand jury charged with fraudulent use of the company's finances. Speaking in his own defence, he wins the jury round to return a verdict of not guilty (even the judge shows his joy), and parades his fifty cars around the square outside the courthouse, while crowds cheer from the sidelines. 'It's the idea that counts, and the dream,' Tucker declares.

If *Peggy Sue Got Married* was spring, *Gardens of Stone* autumn, and *The Godfather Part III* would be winter, then *Tucker* could be seen as summer. Despite its over-idealized Capraesque plot and style, *Tucker* is an affable portrait of an independently-minded go-getter, played with almost unvarying energy by a constantly smiling Jeff Bridges. As in *The Godfather* films, *The Cotton Club* and *Peggy Sue Got Married*, Coppola reveals his brilliance in capturing the essence of an era: mock newsreels, nostalgic tunes like 'Hold That Tiger', rendered almost as the hero's theme song, and a 'Tucker' jingle written by Carmine Coppola. With split screens and some smart cutting, the film has not only the rhythm of a musical, but some of the genre's dreamlike unreality, due in part to the strong design concept of Dean Tavoularis. Tucker and his team getting the car ready for display are like kids determined to put on a show in a barn on time against all the odds. Despite the obstacles in the inventor's way, the film is a bit too sunny for its own good, and some darker shades might have given it more depth. Yet much of the exuberance transmits itself to the audience, highlighting the line in the film, uttered by Martin Landau – a touching hang-dog portrayal – 'If you get too close to people, you catch their dreams.'

Because much of the control of the film was in George Lucas' hands, Coppola felt he was unable to make it as personal as he had hoped. 'I'd lost some of my confidence,' he confided to the *New York Times*. 'I knew George has a marketing sense of what the people might want. He wanted to candy-apple it up a bit, make it like a Disney film. He was at the height of his success, and I was at the height of my failure, and I was a little insecure . . . . I think it's a good movie – it's eccentric, a little wacky, like the Tucker car – but it's not the movie I would have made at the height of my power.' Despite George Lucas' efforts to make sure *Tucker* would gain a wide public, it only had a mediocre success at the box-office.

Nevertheless, *Tucker: The Man and his Dream*, which bore the dedication: 'For Gio, who loved cars', could be considered as Coppola's biography at one remove, a parable of the setting up and demise of Zoetrope. In interview after interview, Coppola strayed from talking of Preston Tucker into talking of himself and his company – his invention that nobody seemed to want.

Tucker tried to manufacture cars in Chicago rather than Detroit; Coppola moved from Los Angeles to San Francisco to make his films away from the big studios; both Tucker and Coppola assembled a close-knit group around them; both were salesmen with the gift of the gab; both gambled on extravagant themes and spent lavishly, sacrificing a great deal to pursue their dreams. In the film, Tucker's wife says of him, 'No matter how much he makes, he always manages to spend twice as much.' Most touching of all the parallels is seen when Tucker's eldest son (Christian Slater) asks if he can stay and work with his father, producing the cars rather than go to college. When Gio was sixteen, he begged Francis to let him leave school and work with him on the movies.

Coppola's family was more important to him than ever, and they had been drawn closer since the death of Gio. He set up Commercial Pictures, a small company for twenty-two-year-old Roman, which would turn out cheap movies on the lines of Corman. The first picture produced by Roman, and directed by Victor Salva, was *Clownhouse*, a horror film about a gang of youths dressed as clowns who terrorize suburban boys.

Although Sofia, now seventeen, had appeared in a few of her father's films, she would gain more experience of movie-making by co-writing a script (with Francis), and designing the costumes and main graphic titles for *Life Without Zoe*, one of three short films in *New York Stories*, the others being by Martin Scorsese and Woody Allen. It was a real family affair, with Carmine composing the music (and making an appearance as a street violinist), Talia in a leading role, and Gia, the newly-born daughter of Jacqueline and Gio, playing Zoe as a baby. The name of the little heroine – 'My parents called me Zoe because it means Life in Greek' – has, of course, another association close to home.

The thirty-four-minute episode follows a spoiled and wealthy twelve-year-old girl (Heather McComb), who lives in the Sherry-Netherland Hotel in Manhattan. Her only companion there is Hector, the butler (Don Novello), because her mother (Talia Shire), a fashion photographer, is seldom at home, and her father (Giancarlo Giannini) is a famous flautist who frequently travels the world. After a fancy-dress party given by 'the richest boy in the world', Zoe and her mother fly to Athens where they watch her father performing in a concert at the Acropolis.

Although *Life Without Zoe* is supposedly set in the present-day, it is stunningly old-fashioned in its attitudes and Shirley Temple story – poor little rich girl brings her parents together. Even New York seems to belong to the 1940s where, as Dean Tavoularis commented, the characters live in 'a kind of Noël Coward-like world for children.' Even taken as a fairy story of a little princess, it is too inconsequential for any serious consideration, and the ending at the Parthenon with mother and daughter cheering the father after his performance, as the orchestra continues to play, is pretty hard to take. But, like *Tucker*, the design concept is dominant, and the children's fancy-dress party is spectacularly staged, although the indulgently viewed kids imitating their parents are rather revolting, as is the uncritical celebration of excessive wealth. *Life Without Zoe* got disastrous reviews when it opened in February 1989, particularly when sandwiched between the powerful Martin Scorsese, and amusing Woody Allen segments. Coppola's career seemed to have lost all sense of direction. Life Without Zoetrope was painful. He needed to make some big money and to get back on track. Where else to look except to the past, when he was at the height of his power and confidence. . . .

17 Twilight of the Godfathers

The Godfather Part III deals with this kind of American family that functions almost like royalty . . . . Michael Corleone's instincts were always to be legitimate, so it would be odd now when he's almost in the King Lear period of his life, if his prime aim and purpose were not indeed to become legitimate. The result is a very classical piece in the tradition of a Shakespeare play.

When Paramount first suggested to Coppola that he make *The Godfather Part III*, he refused. 'I would just take the story and tell it again, which is what they do on these sequels. I'm not really interested in gangsters any more.' Yet, a year later, on 27 November 1989, he embarked on *Part III*.

Why had he changed his mind? The main reason seems to have been money. He was being sued by Jack Singer for $6 million because he had never paid back the $3 million bail-out loan. However, Coppola argued that as Singer had bought Zoetrope for $5 million less than the appraised value, which was less than the debt, he owed nothing. But, on advice that he would most likely lose the case and have to pay up, he signed a lucrative deal with Paramount. He was given a budget of $44 million, with location work in New York, Sicily and Rome, and considerable freedom to make the kind of film he wanted.

Naturally, Al Pacino would resume the role of Michael Corleone, whom Coppola wanted at the centre of the story, which was originally titled *The Death of Michael Corleone*. 'He was a man looking for redemption, asking, "What have I done with my life, what have I done with my family?" I was more interested in the story from that point of view than creating yet another nemesis that Michael outsmarts,' Coppola remarked.

Both Talia Shire and Diane Keaton continued in their characters. Unfortunately, Robert Duvall asked for a fee of $3.5 million to play Tom Hagen again, but the studio was unable to meet it. Yet they were prepared to pay Pacino $2 million more. As a result, Tom Hagen is mentioned as having died. Both Coppola and the critics regretted the absence of this strong unifying character, who would have played an even more impor-

Directing Al Pacino (right) and Andy Garcia in The Godfather
Part III **(1991).**

tant role in the family's fortunes, and found George Hamilton's smooth
lawyer an inadequate substitute.

Gordon Willis returned as cinematographer in order to retain the style
of the previous parts. Frank Sinatra expressed interest in playing
Altobello, the close friend of the Corleones, but he could not fit it into his
schedule (Eli Wallach took the role instead.) Andy Garcia, a thirty-four-
year-old Cuban born actor, won the part of Vincent, the illegitimate son of

Sonny Corleone, who becomes the Don's heir apparent. Madonna tested for the role of the photographer who stalks Michael, but Coppola declared that, at thirty-two, she was too old, and gave it to Bridget Fonda. The nineteen-year-old Winona Ryder was cast in the plum role of Pacino's daughter (Julia Roberts had been first choice but she was busy on *Pretty Woman*), but when Winona arrived in Rome, escorted by boyfriend Johnny Depp, she collapsed from overwork, and was told to rest on doctor's orders. At the last moment, Coppola took a risk and, against the wishes of Paramount executives who wanted a star, gave his eighteen-year-old daughter Sofia the part. Diane Keaton and Al Pacino also protested. Talia Shire, reprising her role of Connie, warned her brother not to put Sofia in the film. 'Francis, don't do this to her. She's not ready.'

Coppola explained: 'Obviously, the kind of daughter I wanted for Michael was my own daughter, because I was thinking, "If I were Michael and I had this nice daughter, she'd be like Sofia. She'd be beautiful, but she wouldn't be movie-star beautiful. She'd be Italian so that in her face you could see Sicily." I saw that Winona was out of it, and I reached out for what I thought could make it work.'

Sofia, who had just finished her first term at college, realized that no matter how good she was, she would be slaughtered. 'Part of me was saying they hate me because I am his kid,' Sofia said, terrified when she started shooting, and was often in tears. She also had qualms about doing love scenes for her father. Predictably, although most of the reviews of *The Godfather Part III* were good, the main negative notes struck were those on Sofia's performance. Coppola felt the criticisms of Sofia were meant for him and that Sofia received them the way Mary Corleone got the bullets intended for Michael. In fact, Sofia, though lacking identifiable star quality, is adequate, and sometimes touching, in the role, and in no way sabotaged the project.

Installed at Cinecittà in Rome, Coppola began shooting what had to be the last chapter of *The Godfather* saga. Ellie recorded in her diary in March 1990: 'Francis was very depressed. He spoke with such conviction about all the things wrong in his life, how he hated that he was doing the same material he had done nearly twenty years ago, how he hated the process of making movies, and all the time it took. He said the only thing he liked about film-making was the technology.'

Despite the experience on *One From The Heart* when the cast and crew felt their director was detached from them, Francis spent a great deal of his time in his Silverfish, the Airstream trailer that followed him everywhere. There he sat for hours watching the video monitors, and using the loudspeakers to convey his instructions to those on the sound stage, his voice booming out like the voice of God.

During the next eight months, in Rome and Sicily, Coppola had to try and get the material on film, and attempt to keep his cast happy. There was tension on the set because Pacino and Diane Keaton, who play husband and wife, broke up their real-life affair in Rome, and more tension between Coppola and his insecure daughter, a nervous Andy Garcia, and the producer Fred Roos, who was coping with budgetary problems. Then there was still some shooting to be done in New York. Pacino was at Coppola's side at every day's viewing of the rushes, and contributed much to the film.

The Godfather Part III begins in 1979. It follows the pattern of its predecessors by starting with a large celebration, during which dirty deals are being made behind closed doors. The Corleone family has amassed unimaginable wealth, and as the film opens Michael, now in his sixties, is being invested with a great honour by the Church. He has spent the last years trying to move the family out of crime into legitimate business for the sake of his daughter Mary (Sofia Coppola). He has turned over a lot of the family rackets to a new generation like Joey Zasa (Joe Mantegna), who deals in drugs, and Sonny's son, Vincent (Andy Garcia), who is keen to eliminate the Corleones' enemies. But Michael is trapped by the past, and cannot escape. On the steps outside the opera house, after a performance of *Cavalleria Rusticana*, in which his son Anthony is the leading tenor, Michael is shot at, but Mary is killed instead.

The conclusion to the Corleone family saga is taken at a much slower, more contemplative pace, although it is no less impressive than the earlier films. Not only had Michael Corleone aged, but both Al Pacino and Francis Coppola were sixteen years older since the previous *Godfather*. Here, the Mafia link with the Catholic Church is not only used to demonstrate how wide corruption spreads, but it also informs the theme of Michael's struggle for redemption from the crimes, including fratricide, that weigh heavily upon him. What we see, however, is an even more violent and unscrupulous new generation, represented by his nephew Vincent.

The finale takes place during a performance of Mascagni's *verismo* opera about a vendetta in a small Sicilian village, the melodramatic events on stage reflecting the escalating tension and violence off it. It is a superlative example of Coppola's use of montage, music, close-up, and sound to create a dramatic effect, and is a fitting climax to a remarkable trilogy. Coppola often resents being always considered 'The Godfather man', but whatever else of quality he has created, nothing has ever equalled the power and the glory of what started as 'just a gangster movie' and ended as one of the great achievements of post-war cinema.

18 Rising from the Grave

I liked that Dracula himself was fascinated with science. I liked the fact that the castle was all propped up with steel, as though he had brought Eiffel there. At the cinematograph, he says, 'How incredible science is!'

When Winona Ryder, whose breakdown prevented her from being in *The Godfather Part III*, brought Coppola a script of *Dracula* by James V. Hart, in which she wanted to play Jonathan Harker's fiancée, Mina, he asked, 'Is it the real Bram Stoker *Dracula* or is it some modern version?' The film, shot at Sony Pictures Studios in San Francisco, was indeed inspired by the original Bram Stoker novel, but carried the author's name in the title because Universal Pictures' ownership of the rights to the title *Dracula*.

Coppola was impressed by the script and changed very little. Jim Hart, a Texan author, who dreamed of writing for the movies, had produced his first-draft script called *Dracula: The Untold Story*, as long ago as 1977. Francis added certain elements to the story, including the venereal disease reference. 'Civilization and syphilization have advanced together,' says Anthony Hopkins as Professor Abraham Van Helsing. Given the bloody theme, there is also an implicit allusion to AIDS.

Coppola was determined to demonstrate that he could make a big, expensive movie and not go over budget. 'I really wanted to solidify a new working base with the Hollywood companies,' he remarked. What, in truth, he wanted was a chance to pour some money back into Zoetrope. Now he had $42 million, with the backing of a large studio. Unfortunately, he was not allowed to work with Vittorio Storaro and Dean Tavoularis because 'Columbia did not want to use the kind of people that traditionally go over budget.' Like *One From The Heart*, the whole of *Dracula* was to be shot on sound stages on which Coppola envisaged the sets and costumes having the symbolist look of Gustav Klimt. Six weeks before shooting began, Coppola fired production designer Dante Ferreti, who was diverging from this conception, and hired Thomas Sanders to take over.

With Anthony Hopkins as Professor Abraham Van Helsing on the set of Bram Stoker's Dracula **(1992).**

For the title role, various names surfaced, including Daniel Day Lewis (but he was busy making *The Last of the Mohicans*), Gabriel Byrne, Antonio Banderas and Armand Assante. But Coppola cast thirty-four-year-old Gary Oldman, because he remembered him from *Sid and Nancy* – 'unattractive raunchy characters but their love was so beautiful and so passionate.'

The cast moved into the large house on the Coppola estate for a week, two days of which was spent reading Bram Stoker's novel aloud. Then they each researched their parts, and improvised lines. 'They were all off researching,' complained Oldman. 'And I'm four hundred years old and dead – how the fuck do I get into that?' However, he did take fencing lessons, and practised his accent, 'Hungarian with a dash of Romanian.' He also dipped rather too regularly into Coppola's wine reserves. Later, during the shooting, Oldman was picked up for drunk driving after a night on the town with Keifer Sutherland, for which he was given a six-month driving ban.

Nonetheless, Oldman gives an unforgettable performance, alternately a crabby, prune-faced aristocrat in an outlandish eighteenth-century wig, veering between smiling, weeping and exploding with rage; a suave, seductive prince, and a grotesque bat-like vampire. His accent, too, is credible Transylvanian, pronouncing his name as Dra-cula. Despite a voice coach, the English accent of Keanu Reeves as Jonathan Harker is as unconvincing as his stiff acting, but Winona Ryder, as his fiancée, has a good shot at the accent, as well as having the perfect looks for the pale Victorian heroine, the object of Dracula's desires.

Bram Stoker's Dracula or, more accurately, Francis Ford Coppola's *Dracula*, is a film that counter-demonstrates the principal that less is more. With all the money involved and the technical wizardry at his fingertips, Coppola went all out for spectacle and special effects. As a result, most of the classic Gothic elements of the novel, or even the earlier, greater Dracula movies such as Carl Dreyer's *Vampyr*, F. W. Murnau's *Nosferatu* and Tod Browning's *Dracula* starring Bela Lugosi, have been surpassed in pyrotechnics and horror, but not in subtlety.

Yet, Coppola makes direct reference to these films by introducing early cinematique techniques – irises, slow fades and dissolves – while using every modern method at his disposal. In an attempt to recapture some of the style of early cinema, Coppola used in-camera opticals. 'We didn't have any money to do a sequence in London,' Coppola explained with reference to the sequence when Dracula first spots Mina, 'So I had this idea that we'd get any street set and photograph it with a Pathé camera to give the feel of old London.'

Coppola obviously wanted to stress the Freudian aspects of the story, linking vampirism and sexuality, most vulgarly in the skin-flick scenes of topless harpies trying to debauch the bland Keanu Reeves in Dracula's castle. These were directed by Roman Coppola, and choreographed by Michael Smuin. Aside from the erotic element, Coppola concentrated on the love story between Dracula and Mina – a sort of *Beauty and the Beast* romance. But there are as many holes in the plot as in the necks: why, for example, does Dracula need an estate agent to negotiate certain properties in London if he has supernatural powers to go anywhere he pleases in whatever form, travelling in space and time? It hardly matters, though, because the most important ingredients in the film are the costumes by Eiko Ishioka and the production design by Thomas Sanders. The special effects *are* special – notably in those scenes shot by Roman Coppola– and most arresting in the different manifestations of Dracula, who, at one stage, becomes a demon straight out of Goya.

Bram Stoker's Dracula took $82 million in the first two months at the US box-office, and brought in much more from all over the world. Coppola began to think big once more. Projects he began to develop included an H. G. Wellsian science fiction film called *Megalopolis*; another on the search for a cure for AIDS. But it took him five years to get another film made, and it was neither of these.

19 Child's Play

I love to be around kids, even liked little kids when I was little, and then I still liked little kids when I was older. At my age now, I have this celebrity that I've achieved, and yet in my heart I don't feel so much different than I did when I was younger. With kids, you're on a one-to-one with them, whereas the adults are always playing you.

In 1992, Coppola planned to make a new version of *Pinocchio*, mixing live-action with cartoon characters. He was hoping to use the drawings of Roberto Innocenti, who had illustrated a version of the Carlo Collodi story a few years previously. What caught Coppola's eye was the highly detailed naturalism of the drawings, with fantasy and reality treated as perfectly normal partners, locating events firmly in Tuscany, where the tale is set. Innocenti, in fact, started sketching for Coppola, but the project fell through. Perhaps he saw something in his next film that related to *Pinocchio*, about a boy puppet who wanted to be like other children.

Eyebrows were raised when, for his return to the screen, he chose a Disney vehicle for Robin Williams. He admitted that the family wine business was of equal importance to making movies. *Jack* was an opportunity to plough his fee back into American Zoetrope, and embark on another grand scheme. 'I support my family with the wine business and if I can make money from the film business I use it to subsidize my personal work. But, although he did *Jack* for the money, he defended it. 'I've always tried different styles. *Peggy Sue Got Married* was a kind of sweet fable, and in a way, *Jack* is like that. Even though *Jack* didn't originate with me I tried to tackle the story with as much feeling and love as I could.'

In the pre-credit sequence, at a fancy-dress party (an adult version of the one in *Life Without Zoe*), a woman dressed as the Wicked Witch of the West, accompanied by her husband, in the costume of the Tin Man, is rushed to hospital to give birth to a baby boy, although she is only two month's pregnant. She is told that the child's inner genetic clock is faster than anyone else's, and that he will age four years for every one. Ten years later, we see him, a lonely child in a forty-year-old man's body, lovingly cared for by his mother and father (Diane Lane and Brian Kerwin).

However, even at the risk of the boy being taunted by other pupils, his private tutor (Bill Cosby) advises Jack's parents to send him to school. At first he is treated as a freak by them ('A six-foot, hairy kid') but, after making a friend of ten-year-old Louie (Adam Zolotin), he gradually becomes 'cool' in his classmates' eyes. When he graduates at seventeen (i.e sixty-eight), he has won the hearts of everyone. In a final speech, the now stooped and grey-haired Jack underlines the film's banal message that we should never forget the child in us all, and that life goes by too quickly for everyone. 'When you see a shooting star, think of me . . . .'

Of all of Coppola's movies, even those that were mere commissions, *Jack* is the least personal, the least interesting and, perhaps, the worst of his films. In fact, it is difficult to believe that the man who made *The Conversation*, *The Godfather* trilogy and *Apocalypse Now* could have been responsible for this conventional product off the Hollywood assembly line. Even with Dean Tavoularis as the production designer, the film has none of the particular Coppola 'look'. *Jack* also gives the lie to the theory that he dropped his middle name on those projects to which he felt no deep commitment. Taking into account the fact that any film directed by Francis Ford Coppola or Francis Coppola still arouses a certain level of expectation, *Jack* would nevertheless have been a bummer if directed by someone of lesser reputation.

Yet, the picture dedicated to his ten-year-old granddaughter Gia (Gian-Carlo's daughter): 'For Gia - "When you see a shooting star . . ."' did contain one personal aspect, as Coppola explained. 'When I was nine I was confined to a room for over a year with polio, and because polio is a child's illness they kept every other kid away from me. I remember being pinned to this bed, and longing for friends and company. When I read *Jack*, I was moved because that was precisely his problem; there are no children in his life.'

The message of the screenplay also struck a chord with him. 'The idea is that it really isn't how long you live, it's how completely you live your life that is important . . . . My son Gio only lived twenty-two years, but it was a complete twenty-two years. He got to do everything - he got to be a kid, he got to be an adult, got to fall in love, got to shoot all that stuff on *The Cotton Club* . . . .'

As *Jack*, Robin Williams does the best he can with the role, though he sometimes verges on the embarrassing. The problem is that Williams always seems to play a ten-year-old no matter what part he is given, both in his wacky and his tearful mode, therefore there seemed no need for Coppola to have made Williams spend three weeks with real ten-year-olds to immerse himself in the role. 'We just ran around up at his place,' said the actor, 'It was great, because you assimilate behaviour without even knowing it.'

Yet Coppola told Williams that he didn't want him to imitate a ten-year-old, he wanted him to discover the ten-year-old within him. More unconventional casting was that of Bill Cosby as Jack's tutor. Cosby, a friend, taught Coppola how to play baccarat and to smoke a cigar. At first, Francis found Cosby difficult to work with because he always arrived on set with strong convictions as to how he was going to play his scenes. But the director managed to persuade him to take other approaches.

Because *Jack* is meant to appeal to ten-year-olds, or adults with the minds of ten-year-olds, it skirts the sexual issue, although *Jack* is made a play for by Louie's tarty mother (Fran Drescher, sexy and funny), and he seems to feel something for his warm, understanding teacher (Jennifer Lopez) – everyone is sickeningly warm and understanding in the picture. Naturally, there is also no hint of paedophilia in the notion that, objectively, it seems rather bizarre for a man with the appearance of a forty-year-old to be always hanging around ten-year-old boys.

Coppola's direction is as competent as ever, though it has little invention: there are obvious touches related to the theme such as time-lapse and speeded-up photography, and a supposedly clever cinéphile joke: when the boys' treehouse is about to collapse, there is a shot of the teetering cabin from Chaplin's *The Gold Rush* on the television, the sort of thing he did much better in *You're A Big Boy Now*, way back in 1967. One would be justified in asking if Coppola was regressing more than progressing, though a study of his snakes-and-ladders career would prevent one from ever judging too soon. Though *Jack* was a snake, any of his next films could very well be a ladder that reaches the heights where reside *The Godfather* trilogy, *The Conversation* and *Apocalypse Now*.

Epilogue

In my life I've only ever made two films that were totally from my original stories
– *The Conversation* and *The Rain People* – and I would very much like to do
that again.

Francis Coppola's latest film to date is *The Rainmaker*, another adaptation
from a bestselling John Grisham novel, a commercial project for which
Paramount was quite happy to put up the money. Marketed as *John
Grisham's The Rainmaker*, rather than Coppola's, it is certainly an entertaining, if not old-fashioned movie on a favourite theme of Hollywood:
small fry taking on some big fish . . . and winning. They don't come smaller
than Danny DeVito, who provides a great deal of comedy as a go-getter
working for a newly-qualified lawyer (the promising young Matt Damon)
out to defeat slick Jon Voight, defending his corrupt insurance broker
clients. Coppola's script retains a certain ironic tone throughout and,
despite being cursory on two of the three cases dealt with, much pleasure
is derived from seeing the underdog have his day. Although rather
impersonal, *The Rainmaker* does echo *Tucker* in this regard, and there is
a particularly poignant scene of a father mourning the death of his son.

The movie had begun shooting in Memphis, Tennessee in October 1996,
and Coppola had brought it in on time and on budget. The battles in which
he had fought every inch to get his own way in everything, and which
earned him the reputation as a prodigal trouble-maker, are long past. The
Hollywood maverick seems to have joined the common herd. But Coppola
still hankers after the days when he could justifiably be called an *auteur*.

The fact is that Coppola can demand a big fee and get a percentage of
the profits of any movie, except for those that originate from him.

Being something of a realist, I understand the current situation of the world
motion-picture industry [he explained to the writer Peter Biskind in 1996]. It's obvious that nobody wants any personal work from me in terms of the industry. I'm
well aware that nobody wants me to do a movie, say, on the scale of *Apocalypse
Now* in terms of substance, with an original script like *The Conversation*, which is

what I feel I should do and want to do. So I guess my feeling is, now that I'm fifty-seven, that perhaps since I don't need the money, and I have realized all the dreams that I could ever want, and I've made my family secure, and we have a wonderful life, that if I make a film like *The Rainmaker*, then I would have the money to make my own film . . . . It would be expensive because I would like to do something ambitious and something that would be sufficiently different . . . . I'd hope to do a bigger film with an original screenplay, certainly by the time I reach sixty. I feel that I owe it to myself to have a shot at something with original writing, where I can use the epic level that I'm capable of . . . . That kind of film, if it was accidentally destroyed in an earthquake in the lab after my death, good or bad, that people would think it was a loss.

It is true that Coppola has realized many of his dreams, though he has seen many of them shattered, such as the Zoetrope ideal of having his own studio where he would be free to make his own movies away from Hollywood. Nevertheless, he has been able to make a number of masterpieces such as *The Godfather* trilogy within the system, and he has never abandoned the philosophy expressed by his hero in *Tucker*: 'It's the idea that counts, and the dream.' There is little doubt that there will be further works on which the credit 'A film by Francis Ford Coppola' will really mean something again.

THE

REVIEWS

YOU'RE A BIG BOY NOW

December 14, 1966

Nutty comedy about a young male virgin; okay for selected situations.

Hollywood, Dec. 9. Seven Arts Pictures release of Phil Feldman production. Stars Elizabeth Hartman, Geraldine Page, Julie Harris, Peter Kastner, Rip Torn; features Michael Dunn, Tony Bill, Karen Black, Dolph Sweet, Michael O'Sullivan. Directed, scripted by Francis Ford Coppola, based on novel by David Benedictus; camera (PatheColor), Andy Laszlo; music, John Sebastian; editor, Aram Avakian; assit. director, Larry Sturhahn. Reviewed at Fine Arts Theatre, Dec. 8, '66. Running Time, 96 mins. (Color)

Barbara Darling	Elizabeth Hartman
Margery Chanticleer	Geraldine Page
Miss Thing	Julie Harris
Bernard	Peter Kastner
I.H. Chanticleer	Rip Torn
Richard Mudd	Michael Dunn
Raef	Tony Bill
Amy	Karen Black
Policeman Francis Graf	Dolph Sweet
Kurt Doughty	Michael O'Sullivan

"You're a Big Boy Now," another in the rising tide of nutty pix, might be gauged a conversation piece in the selected-situation market for which this Phil Feldman production obviously is aimed. It is one of those films with a simple premise – this time a virginal young man growing into manhood, not so much through his own efforts as those about him – which has been expanded glowingly in a sophisticated approach. There probably will be those who object to development of the motivating idea, particularly as it relates to today's mores and morals – perhaps rightfully – but by the same token picture undoubtedly will be hailed by a certain section of the film-going public with enthusiasm.

There can be no doubt that the Seven Arts release is a director's picture. Francis Ford Coppola, according to brochure of credits handed out at preview, wrote and directed "Boy" for his master's thesis at the UCLA Film School, as a student of its Theatre Arts dept. It is thoroughly professional, however, with a cast of top names and a budget said to be around the million-dollar mark, produced entirely in N.Y. Feature is packed with clever touches both in the gag field and in sustained sequences, and Coppola has drawn top-flight performances from his talented cast.

Credit is given in introductory titles to the cooperation of the N.Y. city fathers, along with expressed gratitude to Mayor John Lindsay and the N.Y. Public Library. One may wonder, as story unfolds on a collection of rara avis associated with the library (including the oddball curator of rare books and a booster-sniffing employee), why such cooperation was granted, since the institution citadel of respectability – backdrops much of the action, including young man's introduction to sex. Film runs the gamut of way-out story-telling, characteristic of much current screen humor.

Peter Kastner plays a roller-skating stack boy in the library, somewhat of a dreamer. Against the tearful protests of boy's mother, Geraldine Page, the father, Rip Torn, decides the best way for his son to grow up would be to move out of the family home on his own. Straightway, lad becomes ensconced in a rooming house run by Julie Harris, where the third floor is governed by a rooster belonging to landlady's departed brother and which doesn't like pretty girls.

With the help of his library, dope-inclined pal, Tony Bill, and a pretty library assistant, Karen Black, the boy is launched on his road to manhood, which takes him into the arms of a sexy, way-out, Greenwich Village discotheque dish, Elizabeth Hartman. Frequent laughs spark his career toward full-blossomed virility, with amusing bumps along the way.

Kastner turns in a slick portrayal, endowing role with just the proper emphasis upon youth in the wondering stage. Miss Hartman, who previously scored so heavily in "Patch of Blue," scores again in a vastly different type of role, to which she gives full conviction.

Both Miss Page as the mother and Miss Harris as the landlady go all-out in hilarious roles and Torn, too, delivers a sock [good] performance as the father who has difficulty understanding his son. Miss Black offers a sensitive enactment of the girl in love with Kastner and Bill is arresting as the pal. Excellent support also is offered by Dolph Sweet as a cop in the rooming house, and Michael Dunn as Miss Hartman's friend.

Technical credits all rate high, standouts here Andy Laszlo's color photography, John Sebastian's music score, Vassele Fotopoulos' art direction and Aram Avakian's editing.

Whit.

FINIAN'S RAINBOW

October 9, 1968

Film version of 1947 Broadway musical hit shapes as good box-office escapism. Roadshow created at modest cost by W7. Racial and other topical spoofing plus strong cast all pluses.

Hollywood, Aug. 28. Warner Bros.-Seven Arts release of Joseph Landon production. Stars Fred Astaire, Petula Clark. Directed by Francis Ford Coppola. Screenplay, E.Y. Harburg, Fred Saidy, based on their play; camera (Technicolor), Philip Lathrop; editor, Melvin Shapiro; music, Burton Lane; lyrics, Harburg; production design, Hilyard M. Brown; sound, M. A. Merrick, Dan Wallin; assit. director, Fred Gammon. Reviewed at Pacific's Pantages Theatre, L.A., Aug. 27 '68. Running Time (excluding intermission), 145 mins. (Panavision – color – songs)

Finian McLonergan	Fred Astaire
Sharon McLonergan	Petula Clark
Og, The Leprechaun	Tommy Steele
Woody Mahoney	Don Francks
Judge Rawkins	Keenan Wynn
Susan The Silent	Barbara Hancock
Howard	Al Freeman, Jr.
Buzz Collina	Ronald Colby
Sheriff	Dolph Sweet
District Attorney	Wright King
Henry	Louil Silas

Though tradescreened Aug. 27 this review appears only now on dictated publication date.

A blending of older and younger talent, both before and behind the camera, has translated "Finian's Rainbow," the 1947 hit legituner [stage musical], into pleasant, entertaining 1969 screen escapism for the entire family. Fred Astaire and Petula Clark star in writer

Joseph Landon's maiden film production, in which a young director Francis Ford Coppola & vet choreographer Hermes Pan have worked capably to sustain a light, pastoral musical fantasy. Topicality of civil rights angles, underscored by comedy values in the E.Y. Harburg-Fred Saidy book and screenplay, and the many memorable Burton Lane melodies which have become standards, should produce some sunny b.o. (box office) results for the Warner Bros.-Seven Arts release.

When film's budget was disclosed last year to the N.Y. financial community, some eyebrows were raised that a road-show fantasy could be brought in for a projected $4,000,000. It is understood that exact final cost is under this figure. Whatever the reason – perhaps the five weeks of intense rehearsal preceding the seven weeks of principal photography, film has realized on screen a very large proportion of its investment, a very strong asset.

Overall, film has an ethereal quality: it's a blend of real elements, such as love, greed, compassion, prejudice, and other aspects of human nature both noble and otherwise; yet it's also infused with mystical elements of magic, leprechauns, pixies and wishes that come true. In a less turbulant real world, film would appear as outright fantasy with a prominent strain of social consciousness. As things are today, however, it seems more like a very strong message pic, mitigated with elements of fantasy.

Filming concept has realized the apparent desire to exist in a twilight zone: modern cinematic techniques lend a low-key dramatic atmosphere to the pic, in opposition to the sometimes stark plot twists and turns; the fluid integration of musical numbers – which constitute over one-third of the footage – is a constant reminder that Rainbow Valley is both real and unreal; the submerging of players into the dramatic fabric, instead

of the film being a "personality vehicle," also manifests the evident concept.

End result is a partial escapism, which will prove as rewarding to those who believe in dreams as it may be fulfilling to those who have never been able to afford the luxury of dreaming.

Following a 90-second overture, film opens leisurely with Astaire and Miss Clark, his daughter, on a montage tour of the U.S. as the Phil Norman-Westheimer Co. titles waft appropriately across the Panavision-Technicolor screen. The stars come to rest in Rainbow Valley, just as the police henchmen of racist judge Keenan Wynn are about to foreclose on property owned by vagabond Don Francks. Astaire bails out Francks, and latter's romance with Miss Clark develops. Tommy Steele, top-featured, arrives as the leprechaun searching for gold which Astaire has stolen.

The major plot angle is race prejudice, and in the casting of Wynn has come the film's most outstanding performance. He is not a sympathetic character, but Wynn makes the part at least understandable and pitiable. The laugh highlight, in a film which generally aims for quiet chuckles and smiles, is when Al Freeman, Jr., an educated Negro botanist, tongue-in-cheeks the cliche "shuffling" Negro stereotype for Wynn's irritated benefit.

Miss Clark invoking 1 of 3 magic wishes, turns Wynn black, who thereupon garners an appreciation of what prejudice is all about. Wynn's work here, expansive yet controlled, is superlative. Miss Clark's travail as a suspected witch, Steele's eventual decision to become all-human, for the love of Barbara Hancock, as Susan the Silent, restored to speech, the fade-out marriage of Miss Clark and Francks and Astaire's heart-tugging departure, round out the principal story resolutions.

The Lane melodies, and Harburg lyrics, abound in the frequent production numbers. With "Necessity" the only apparent withdrawal from the original play tune-bank, a host of remembered songs remain, a bumper crop of standards from any show score. "That Old Devil Moon," "How Are Things In Glocca Morra?" "Look To The Rainbow," "If This Isn't Love," and "When I'm Not Near The Girl I Love" are received with great impact.

Also, the lesser-known, but plot-enhancing "Something Sort of Grandish," "That Great Come-And-Get-It Day," "This Time Of The Year," "When The Idle Poor Become The Idle Rich," and the amusing "Begat" song.

Overall pacing is deliberately placid; in first part, which runs just over 89 minutes, major establishing sequences are separated by fades, which stand out all the more as demarcations in light of current jump cuts. Coppola remained true to the overall concept in maintaining a uniform flow. Editing was executed by Melvin Shapiro, and second act runs nearly 56 minutes, including brief overture and recessional. Excluding intermish, total time is 145 minutes.

Astaire's likeability remains undiminished. His big terp [dance] spotlighting comes in the "Idle Rich" sequence, which, at the tradeshow, did not reveal much of his famed footwork. Producer Landon explained that screen masking details had to be ironed out, so that situation presumably is resolved. Miss Clark, in her American film debut, has a winsome charm, which comes through despite a somewhat reactive role. Steele's dynamism is a carryover from legit [theatre], and his screen niche appears to be in broad character cameos.

Miss Hancock, introduced herein, also comes across as a delicate personality, inherently limited of course by the physical handicap parameters of the role. Francks has a solid professional base in niteries [night clubs], tv and legit, and screen potential seems there in light romantic roles. Freeman looks like a solid bet for shy-guy roles, with or without comedy; in serious dramatics, he already has proven himself in Leroi Jones' "Dutchman," both on stage and in the British-made indie film version.

On the technical side, Hilyard M. Brown's exellent production design sustains the mixed fantasy-reality mood desired. Fact that Rainbow Valley was created on the studio backlot is not apparent. Philip Lathrop's superior photography covers the dramatic spectrum, while Dorothy Jeakins' costumes are most colorful and dramatically pertinent to the characters. Ray Heindorf's musical supervision, with assistant Ken Darby, is very good. Joel Freeman, in his last associate producer assignment before coming into his own as a full producer, rates mention for his work here.

Remaining technical credits are excellent.

Murf.

THE RAIN PEOPLE

June 25, 1969

Heavy, slowpaced drama following a runaway pregnant married woman who picks up a brain-damaged but basically gentle hitchhiker.

Freeport, Bahamas, June 15. Warner-Bros.-Seven Arts release of Coppola Co. presentation, produced by Bart Patton and Ronald Colby. Features James Caan, Shirley Knight, Robert Duvall. Written and directed by Francis Ford Coppola. Camera (Technicolor), Wilmer Butler; editor, Blackie Malkin; music, Ronald Stein; art, Leon Ericksen; assistant directors, Richard Bennett, Jack Cunningham; sound, Nathan Boxer. Reviewed at Columbus Theatre, Freeport, Bahamas, June 15 '69. MPAA rating: R. Running Time, 101 mins. (Color)

Kilgannon	James Caan
Natalie	Shirley Knight
Gordon	Robert Duvall
Rosalie	Marya Zimmet
Mr. Alfred	Tom Aldredge
Ellen	Laurie Crews
Artie	Andrew Duncan
Marion	Margaret Fairchild
Beth	Sally Gracie
Lou	Alan Manson
Vinny	Robert Modica

Writer-director Frances Ford Coppola, scrutinizing the flight of a neurotic young woman and her efforts to assist a brain-damaged ex-football player, has developed an overlong, brooding film whose potential b.o. [box office] attraction depends on performances, some excellent photography, and any interest in fatalism. Often lingering too long on detail to build effects, he manages to lose character sympathy.

Producers Bart Patton and Ronald Colby spared nothing in their attempts to provide Coppola's concept every advantage. Film was shot on location cross-country from New York to Colorado, offering a sense of reality and, at the same time, distracting attention.

Shirley Knight, in a neurotic panic because she dreads the ties of domesticity, runs away from her Long Island home and husband. She phones him from the Pennsylvania Turnpike to tell him she is pregnant and has to get away from home for "five minutes – half a day – I don't know!" She picks up James Caan, an ex-football hero whose brain was damaged in a college game, who is hitch-hiking to West Virginia to work for the father of a girlfriend from school. The father is agreeable, but the daughter is embarrassed by the athlete's retardation and demands that he leave. Miss Knight packs him into her station wagon and sets off to find him a job. She manages to place him as a handyman in a roadside reptile farm, drives off in a hurry to get away from Caan and her own sympathy for him, and is arrested for speeding by a cop, Robert Duvall. The local justice of the peace turns out to be the sadistic owner of the reptile farm, who has taken $1,000 the college had given Caan as a payoff. Caan, in Miss Knight's absence, has turned loose some fowl which the owner has been mistreating, and who, when the girl and Duvall arrive, holds back $800 for damages.

Duvall takes the girl to his trailer, the girl rejects him, and Caan breaks in. The immediate tragedy solves Miss Knight's problems in relation to Caan, but her own neuroses are left to be dealt with.

Miss Knight turns in a striking performance, as does Duvall. Caan is saddled with a role that is more robot than retarded, copes as best he can, or anyone could, Marya Zimmet, as Duvall's 12-year-old daughter, flashes briefly, and Tom Aldredge's zoo owner is a strong point.

Wilmer Butler's lensing is excellent, and Ronald Stein's music backs up well. Blackie Malkin's editing is sharp, but the overall mood of the film is depressing. Coppola has created a tour de force that is based on a losing battle from the beginning.

Tone.

THE GODFATHER

March 8, 1972

Powerhouse pre-sell of gangland tale alone assures boxoffice. Two strong performances, good production values. Must open big and mop-up.

Hollywood, Feb. 7 Paramount Pictures release of Albert S. Ruddy production. Stars Marlon Brando. Directed by Francis Ford Coppola. Screenplay, Mario Puzo, Coppola, based on Puzo's novel; camera (Technicolor) Gordon Williams; editors, William Reynolds, Peter Zinner; production designer, Dean Tavoularis; art director, Warren Clymer; set decorator, Philip Smith; costumes, Anna Hill Johnstone; makeup, Dick Smith, Philip Rhodes; special effects, A. D. Flowers, Joe Lombardi, Sass Bedig; assit. director, Fred Gallo; music Nino Rota, conducted by Carlo Savina. Reviewed at Paramount Pictures Studio, Hollywood, Feb. 6 '72. (MPAA Rating: R). Running time: 175 mins. (Color)

Don Vito Corleone	Marlon Brando
Michael Corleone	Al Pacino
Sonny Corleone	James Caan
Clemenza	Richard Castellano
Tom Hagen	Robert Duvall
McCluskey	Sterling Hayden
Jack Woltz	John Marley
Barzini	Richard Conte
Kay Adams	Diane Keaton
Sollozzo	Al Lettieri
Tessio	Abe Vigoda
Connie Rizzi	Talia Shire
Carlo Rizzi	Gianni Russo
Fredo Corleone	John Cazale
Cuneo	Rudy Bond
Johnny Fontana	Al Martino
Mama Corleone	Morgana King
Luca Brasi	Lenny Montana
Paulie Gatto	John Martino
Bonasera	Salvatore Corsitto

Neri	Richard Bright
Moe Greene	Alex Rocco
Bruno Tattaglia	Tony Giorgio
Nazorine	Vito Scotti
Theresa Hagen	Tora Livrano
Phillip Tattaglia	Victor Rendina
Lucy Mancini	Jeannie Linero
Sandra Corleone	Julie Gregg
Mrs. Clemenza	Ardell Sheridan
Apollonia	Simonetta Stefanelli
Fabrizio	Angelo Infanti
Don Tommasino	Corrado Gaipa
Calo	Franco Citti
Vitelli	Saro Urzi

With several million hardcover and paperback books acting as trailers, Paramount's film version of Mario Puzo's sprawling gangland novel, "The Godfather," has a large pre-sold audience. This will bolster the potential for the film which has an outstanding performance by Al Pacino and a strong characterization by Marlon Brando in the title role. It also has excellent production values, flashes of excitement and a well-picked cast.

But it is also overlong at about 175 minutes (played without intermission), and occasionally confusing. While never so placid as to be boring, it is never so gripping as to be superior screen drama. This should not mar Paramount's box office expectations in any measure, though some filmgoers may be disappointed.

Francis Ford Coppola directed the Albert S. Ruddy production, largely photographed in New York. Dean Tavoularis was production designer and Gordon Willis cinematographer (Technicolor) for the handsome visual environment, which besides World War II and postwar styles and props, is made further intriguing by some sort of tinting effect. There are people under 40 who grew up in the period of the film and who recall such color tones as evocative of 20 years earlier, that is, the end of the roaring '20s and the depression. Evidently the artistic effect here is to show some sort of antiquity which no longer exists.

Puzo and Coppola are credited with the adaptation which best of all gives some insight into the origins and heritage of that segment of the population known off the screen (but not on it) as the Mafia or Cosa Nostra. Various ethnic countercultures are part of the past and part of the present, and the judgement of criminality is in part based on the attitudes of the outside majority. Nobody ever denied that a sense of family, cohesion and order are integral, positive aspects of such subgroups; it's just the killing and slaughter that upsets the outsiders.

In "The Godfather," we have the New York-New Jersey world, ruled by five "families," one of them headed by Brando. This was a world where emotional ties are strong, loyalties are somewhat more flexible at times, and tempers are short. In makeup and physical movement instantly evocative of Orson Welles as Charles Foster Kane in "Citizen Kane," Brando does an admirable job as the lord of this domain. He is not on screen for much of the film, though his presence hovers over all of it.

It is Pacino, last seen (by too few) in "Panic in Needle Park," who makes the smash impression here. Initially seen as the son whome Brando wanted to go more or less straight (while son James Caan was to become part of the organization), Pacino matures under trauma of an assassination attempt on Brando, his own double-murder revenge for that on corrupt cop Sterling Hayden and rival gangster Al Lettieri, the counter-vengeance murder of his Sicilian bride, and a series of other personal readjustments which at fadeout find him king of his own mob.

In a lengthy novel filled with many characters interacting over a period of time, readers may digest the passing parade in convenient sittings. But in a film, the audience is forced to get it all at one time. Thus, it is incumbent on filmmakers to isolate, heighten and emphasize for clarity the handfull of key characters; some of that has been done here, and some of it hasn't. The biggest achievement here is the establishment of mood and time.

Among the notable performances are Robert Duvall as Hagen, the non-Italian number-two man is finally stripped of authority after long years of service; Richard Castellano as a loyal follower; John Marley as a Hollywood film mogul pressured into giving a comeback film role (in a war film) to Al Martino, an aging teenage idol; Richard Conte as one of Brando's malevolent rivals; Diane Keaton as Pacino's early sweetheart, later second wife; Abe Vigoda as an eventual traitor to Pacino; Talia Shire as Brando's daughter, married to a weak and traitorous husband, Gianni Russo; John Cazale, another son who moved to Las Vegas when that area attracted the mob, including Alex Rocco as another recognizable character; Morgana King as Brando's wife; and Lenny Montana as a mobster.

Nino Rota's fine score, plus several familiar pop tunes of the periods, further enhanced the mood, and all the numerous technical production credits are excellent. So, at the bottom line, the film has a lot of terrific mood, one great performance by Pacino, an excellent character seque by Brando, and a strong supporting cast. That will be enough for some, only half the job for others.

Murf.

THE CONVERSATION

April 3, 1974

Outstanding, topical crime suspenser. Needs slow sell.

Hollywood, March 27. Paramount Pictures release. Written, produced and directed by Francis Ford Coppola. Stars Gene Hackman. Camera (Technicolor), Bill Butler; editors, Walter Murch, Richard Chew; music, David Shire; production design, Dean Tavoularis; set decoration, Doug von Koss; sound, Walter Murch, Art Rochester, Nat Boxer, Mike Evje; asst. director, Chuck Myers. Reviewed at Paramount Studios, L.A., March 26, '74. (MPAA Rating: PG.) Running Time: 113 mins. (Color)

Harry Caul	Gene Hackman
Stanley	John Cazale
Bernie Moran	Allen Garfield
Mark	Frederic Forrest
Ann	Cindy Williams
Paul	Michael Higgins
Meredith	Elizabeth MacRae
Amy	Teri Garr
Martin Stett	Harrison Ford
Receptionist	Mark Wheeler
The Mime	Robert Shields
Lurleen	Phoebe Alexander
The Director	Robert Duvall

Francis Ford Coppola's "The Conversation" is an excellent film. Written five or more years ago, yet as timely as Watergate, this superb story stars Gene Hackman as a professional surveillance expert whose resurgent conscience involves him in murder and leads to self-destruction. Besides being something of an audio equivalent to Antonioni's "Blow Up," the San Francisco-lensed film ranks with the best of Hitchcock and Clouzot. The outstanding soundtrack collage, so integral to the film's impact, virtually demands that the Paramount release establish itself first in more intimate, sophisticated situations before hitting the general market.

The film was made for The Directors Company, the Paramount affiliate which embraces Coppola, Peter Bogdanovich and William Friedkin. Coppola's own American Zoetrope unit in S.F. did the actual lensing. Fred Roos reunites with Coppola for the fifth time, this time as coproducer.

There are those at the old Seven Arts, and later at the Warner Bros.-Seven Arts, who remember Coppola's desire to film this story, conceived long before governmental and industrial eavesdropping scandals entered the mainstream of public cynicism. The dramatic environment is totally credible in today's atmosphere; five years ago, the film might have been considered science fiction.

Coppola's story is a superior blend of character study and advancing plot. Hackman is fully portrayed as one of those emotion-numbed buggers, for hire to anyone with the price, who combine a pitiably terrifying set of simplistic moral values with go-getting technical expertise. He is introduced in S.F.'s Union Square at midday, teamed with John Cazale and Michael Higgins in tracking the movements and voices of Frederic Forrest and Cindy Williams. The cleaned-up sound tapes, along with the photographs, are to be delivered to a mysterious businessman, played in an unbilled part by Robert Duvall.

What appears to be a simple case of marital infidelity suddenly shifts to a possible murder plot. Hackman, previously cold to the harm he has done to his earlier victims, becomes suspicious when Duvall's executive assistant, Harrison Ford, demands the tapes and photos in lieu of personal delivery to Duvall. Hackman begins listening again to the tapes, and this evidence of late-blooming conscience eventually triggers his own downfall.

Intercut with the deliberately slow

unveiling of the main plot line are Hackman's personal relations. Mistress Teri Garr can no longer stand the mystery of her lovers public life; surveillance competitor Allen Garfield (in another outstanding characterization) caroms [swings] between chumminess and bitter envy; and Elizabeth MacRae, ostensibly a warm-hearted party girl, turns out to be one of Ford's spies sent to steal the material Hackman will not deliver.

Accelerating to its climax, the story resolves with a dreamed murder becoming reality, but the victim is not whom one expected. At fadeout, Hackman must face the future knowing he is himself being tracked; after wrecking his apartment in a vain attempt to find the electronic gear spying on him, Hackman is last seen sitting in the debris, playing his saxophone solos to recorded jazz music, while a pan-and-scan hidden camera mocks him and stalks him.

A major artistic asset to the film – besides script, direction and the top performances of all players – is supervising editor Walter Murch's sound collage and re-recording. Voices come in and out of aural focus in a superb tease. David Shire's piano score is haunting in its simplicity, and is occasionally heightened by a very low frequency tone which subtly raises the blood pressure of an audience. Interspersed to good background effect are some old standards from Paramount's music library.

Production designer Dean Tavoularis, cameraman Bill Butler and set decorator Doug von Koss are noted among the excellent technical credits. At 113 minutes, the film is just about right for its impact. There's no sex and no indiscreet violence, but Coppola makes the adrenalin flow at measured and controlled rates. This is Coppola's most complete, most assured and most rewarding film to date, and the years it took to bring to the screen should be considered well worth the persistence.   *Murf.*

THE GODFATHER, PART II

December 11, 1974

Masterful sequel, broadening story scope of original blockbuster. Outstanding in all respects.

Hollywood, Dec. 9. Paramount Pictures release of a Francis Ford Coppola production. Produced and directed by Coppola. Coproduced by Gray Frederickson, Fred Roos. Features entire cast. Screenplay, Coppola, Mario Puzo, based on Puzo's novel; camera (Technicolor), Gordon Willis; production designer, Dean Tavoularis; editors, Peter Zinner, Barry Malkin, Richard Marks; costumes, Theadora Van Runkle; music, composed by Nino Rota; conducted by Carmine Coppola; art director, Angelo Graham; set decorator, George R. Nelson; assit. directors, Newton Arnold, Henry J. Lange Jr., Chuck Myers, Mike Kusley; Alan Hopkins, Burt Bluestein; special effects, A.D. Flowers, Joe Lombardi; unit publicist, Eileen Peterson. Reviewed in Hollywood, Dec. 9, '74. (MPAA Rating – R). Running Time: 200 mins. (Color)

Michael	Al Pacino
Tom Hagen	Robert Duvall
Kay	Diane Keaton
Vito Corleone	Robert De Niro
Fredo Corleone	John Cazale
Connie Corleone	Talia Shire
Hyman Roth	Lee Strasberg
Frankie Pentangeli	Michael V. Gazzo
Senator Pat Geary	G.D. Spradlin
Al Neri	Richard Bright
Fanutti	Gaston Moschin
Rocco Lampone	Tom Rosqui
Young Clemenza	B. Kirby Jr.
Genco	Frank Sivero
Young Mama Corleone	
	Francesca deSapio

Mama Corleone	Morgana King
Deanna Corleone	Mariana Hill
Signor Roberto	Leopoldo Trieste
Johnny Ola	Dominic Chianese
Michael's bodyguard	Amerigo Tot
Merle Johnson	Troy Donahue
Young Tessio	John Aprea
Tessio	Abe Vigoda
Theresa Hagen	Tere Livrano
Carlo	Gianni Russo
Willi Cicci	Joe Spinell
Vito's mother	Maria Carta
Vitor Andolini (as boy)	Oreste Baldini
Don Francesco	Guiseppe Sillato
Don Tommasino	Mario Cotone
Anthony Corleone	James Gounaris
Marcia Roth	Fay Spain
FBI Man 1	Harry Dean Stanton
FBI Man 2	David Baker
Impresario	Ezio Flagello
Questadt	Peter Donat
Senator 2	Roger Corman
Sonny	James Caan

"The Godfather, Part II" far from being a spinoff followup to its 1972 progenitor is an excellent epochal drama in its own right providing bookends in time – the early part of this century and the last two decades – to the earlier story. Al Pacino again is outstanding as Michael Corleone, successor to the crime family leadership.

The $15,000,000-plus production about 2½ times the cost of the original was most handsomely produced and superbly directed by Francis Ford Coppola who also shares credit for a topnotch script with original book author Mario Puzo. The Paramount release has everything going for it to be an enormous b.o. [box office] winner.

There should be very few criticisms that the latest film glorifies criminality since the script never lets one forget for very long that Pacino as well as Robert De Niro, excellent as the immigrant Sicilian who became the crime family chief as played by Marlon Brando in the first pic., and all their aides are callous, selfish and undeserving of either pity or adulation. Yet, at the same time, there's enough superficial glory in the panoramic story structure to satisfy the demands of less discriminating filmgoers. Hence Coppola has straddled the potential audience and therefore maximized the commercial potential.

The film's 200 minutes to be played without an intermission could be broken down into two acts and 10 scenes. The scenes alternate between Pacino's career in Nevada gambling rackets from about 1958 on and De Niro's early life in Sicily and New York City. A natural break comes after 126 minutes when De Niro involved with low level thievery brutally assassinates Gaston Moschin the neighborhood crime boss without a shred of conscience. It's the only shocking brutality in the film. The small number of other killings are discreetly shot and edited and it makes its point.

Of course, in the modern day sequences, Pacino is also making the point clear that he has passed completely from the idealistic youth that made him enlist in the early days of World War II. A brief flashback scene presents James Caan in a cameo encore as the original heir apparent to his final destiny. In the Caan flashback Pacino is sitting alone with his untested ideals; in the fadeout scene he is again alone, but it's all his own doing.

Brando is said to have accepted the original title role because he considered organized crime a perfect analogy to big business. In the script the analogy is even clearer, especially the pre-Castro Cuban sequences where big business and big crime have a cozy relationship with the former Cuban regime.

Shot on many U.S. and foreign locations, the film had a firstrate technical staff, Gordon Willis encoring superbly as cinematographer. Production designer Dean Tavoularis and associates editors Peter Zinner, Barry Malkin, Richard Marks, costumer Theodora Van Runkle whose fine work had to span decades of changing styles, makeup artists Dick Smith and Charles Schram are equally superior in making just the right changes in features to keep up with the calender and Walter Murch for outstanding sound mixing and montage. Gray Frederickson and Fred Roos share coproducer credit.

The alternating period stories advance smoothly through the many prominent characters all perfectly cast. Performer Robert Duvall is back in top form as the family lawyer, Pacino's only steadfast friend, but a near curtain vibration [end-of- film moment] find him going at last onto that never ending enemies list which Pacino's own machinations inevitably spawn the nurture. Diane Keaton is compelling as Pacino's wife who finally cannot endure life. John Cazale provides a wonderful depth to the weaker brother Fredo whose insecurities set him up for betrayal of Pacino.

Good as Fredo's slatternly wife is Mariana Hill. Talia Shire, as sister Connie, the bride of the first film, later is a hardened and compulsively self destructive jet setter with Troy Donahue in tow for a fling. She finally comes home to be a penitent and surrogate mother of Pacino's children.

An unusual but showmanly casting is that of Actors Studio's Lee Strasberg as an aging but still powerful Jewish crime kingpin. Fay Spain does nicely as his wife as does Dominic Chianese as his top side. Another offbeat casting is that of playwright Michael V. Gazzo returning to acting as an oldtime mobster who later becomes an informer for FBI probes of crime. Gazzo's performance has the right mixture of old world manners that fail to keep step with the times. G.D. Spradlin is excellent as a U.S. Senator whose brothel kinkiness makes him a perfect setup for compromise.

Further offbeat casting comes in a running sequence of a Congressional hearing, one of those periodic public pageants designed to appease middle class uproar over crime. Veteran screenwriter William Bowers is sensational as the crusty chairman while producers Phil Feldman and Roger Corman, the latter an early employer of Coppola, do well as probing senators.

Morgana King again graces the role of Pacino's mother while Francesca deSapio is quietly appealing as the mother in DeNiro's time. Richard Bright and Tom Rosqui are good as Pacino's bodyguards while Amerigo Tot is chilling as Pacino's executioner on the Cuban visit where Strasberg plans Pacino's murder.

Leopoldo Trieste has a marvelous role as a slum landlord, an early victim of DeNiro's growing influence who squirms to the right cues. There are lots of other players filling out the cast.

The excellent score is by Nino Rota conducted by Carmine Coppola who also is credited for incidental additional music. Newspaperman Ed Guthman gets credit for advising on the Congressional hearing sequences. Caan's brief appearances is called a special participation in the crawl [end credits]. All credits come at the end, as in the original film. The R rating is also a repeat, but this film seems less crudely violent in deed, and not in word.

Paramount some weeks ago said it had $26,000,000 in exhibitor advances and guarantees for "Part II," about enough to get it off the nut right away and it looks like the money will be expeditiously earned from a strong b.o. [box office] tide since the "Godfather" exceeded anybodys widest expectations with about $129,000,000 ($87,000,000

domestic) in world film rentals from theatres. There's just no point in gauging the success of "Part II" by comparing or even guessing at the ultimate numbers.

Coppola was in total control of "Part II" and between him and his close associates has been demonstrated the versatility to handle both panoramic scope and personal intimacy the widespread location shooting and post production centres undoubtedly contributed some of the budget overage from the original target of about $12,000,000.

Murf.

APOCALYPSE NOW

May 16, 1979

Powerful war drama. Coppola recon-
firmed as a film creator though latter
portion of film goes fuzzily "literary" and
may hamper audience appeal

**Hollywood, May 12. United Artists release
of a Francis Coppola production.
Produced and directed by Francis
Coppola. Features entire cast.
Coproduced by Fred Roos, Gray
Frederickson. Screenplay, John Milius,
Francis Coppola, based on Joseph
Conrad's "Heart of Darkness"; camera
(Technicolor), Vittorio Storaro; editor,
Barry Malkin; production design, Dean
Tavoularis; art direction, Angelo Graham;
set decoration, Bob Nelson; sound, Jacob
Jacobsen; assit. director, Tony Brandt. No
other credits available. Reviewed at Bruin
Theatre, Westwood, Cal., May 11, 1979.
(No MPAA Rating). Running time: 139
mins. (Color).**

Col. Kurtz	Marlon Brando
Captain Willard	Martin Sheen
Lt. Col. Kilgore	Robert Duvall
Chef	Fred Forrest
Lance	Sam Bottoms
Chief	Albert Hall
Clean	Larry Fishborne
Photo-journalist	Dennis Hopper
Also: Harrison Ford, G.D Spradlin, Bill	
Graham, Cynthia Wood, Francis Coppola.	

"Apocalypse Now" was worth the wait.
Alternately a brilliant and bizarre film,
Francis Coppola's four-year "work in
progress" offers the definitive validation
to the old saw "war is hell." Coppola's
vision of Hell-on-Earth hews closely to
Joseph Conrad's novella, "Heart of
Darkness," and therein lies the film's
principal commercial defect. An exhilarat-
ing action-adventure exercise for two-
thirds of its 139 minutes, "Apocalypse"
abruptly shifts to surrealistic symbolism
for its denouement. Result will be many
spectators left in the lurch, a factor that
won't help in recouping the $50,000,000
or more necessary for break-even by
distrib United Artists, Coppola and the
worldwide distribs involved.

"Apocalyse Now" will also have trouble avoiding political pigeon-holing,
since it's the first film to directly excori-
ate U.S. involvement in the Indochina
war. To be sure, inhumane attitudes
surfaced on both sides as inevitable
consequences of a misunderstood conflict,
but Coppola wields a wide tarbrush
in painting Americans as either "conspira-
torial" or "homicidal," with no one in
between.

Thus, it seems ironic that the most
widely heralded production of the last 10
years may find its niche co-opted by a pic
dealing with a common subject, the effect
of the Vietnam conflict on its participants, "The Deer Hunter" and
"Apocalypse Now" are widely differing
treatments in tone and viewpoint, but in
the eyes of the filmgoing public, if you've
seen one Vietnam war pic, you might
have seen them all.

Which possible reaction would be a
shame, because Coppola here reaffirms
his stature as a top filmmaker.
"Apocalypse Now" takes realistic cinema
to a new extreme – Coppola virtually
creates World War III onscreen.

There are no models or miniatures, no
tank work, nor process screens for the
airborne sequences. The resulting
footage outclasses any war pic made to
date. Coppola's wisest decision was to
narrow his focus on the members of the
patrol boat crew entrusted with taking
Intelligence assassin Martin Sheen on a
hazardous mission up-river into
Cambodia. There Sheen hopes to track
down and "terminate with extreme prejudice" Marlon Brando, a megalomaniac

officer whose methods and motives have become, in Pentagonese, "unsound," as he leads an army of Montagnard tribesmen on random genocide missions.

Interaction of Sheen and the two black (Albert Hall, Larry Fishborne) and two white (Fred Forrest and Sam Bottoms) seamen gives "Apocalypse" a narrative flow when, in fact, there's very little narrative (Sheen has a sporadic voice-over commentary done in groggy sotto-voce that does little to explicate the action).

Robert Duvall appears mid-way as an expansive screen character, an air cavalry helicopter commander who's a surfing nut, and has his boys riding the waves in the midst of flak attacks. These and some other-worldly, nighttime river excursions seem the principal contributions of original scenarist John Milius (who now shares screenwriting credit with Coppola), and they contain a wacky, manic energy that serves "Apocalypse" well.

It's when the ghost of novelist Joseph Conrad enters the picture, and when Milius and Coppola in effect take a back seat to a literary homage, that "Apocalypse Now" runs aground. Despite Vittorio Storaro's haunting imagery, Barry Malkin's explosive editing, and Dean Tavoularis' eerie production design, final third of the pic fails to jell.

Experience is almost a psychedelic one – unfortunately, it's someone else's psyche, and without a copy of crib notes for the Conrad novel, today's mass audience may be hard put to understand just what is going on, or intended.

Marlon Brando's intimidating but inscrutable performance and the bald-headed Colonel Kurtz (named after Conrad's character in "Heart Of Darkness") doesn't clarify anything.

Rest of the cast is extraordinary, with Sheen extremely effective in laconic style, and Forrest, Hall, Fishburne and Bottoms superb in their respective delineations.

Coppola himself shows up in a brief cameo as a combat director, and Bill Graham, Harrison Ford and G.D. Spradlin have minor roles. Duvall gives one of the best characterizations of his career as the surfer commander, and Dennis Hopper is effectively "weird" as Brando's official photographer.

"Apocalypse Now" is emblazoned with firsts: a 70m presentation without credits, a director putting himself personally on the hook for the film's $18,000,000 cost overrun, and then obtaining rights to the pic in perpetuity, and a revolutionary sound system that adds immeasurably to the film's impact.

Even if Coppola isn't haunted by the spectre of financial fiascos like "Cleopatra," there's no assured future for "Apocalypse." It's a complex, demanding, highly intelligent piece of work, coming into a marketplace that does not always embrace those qualities.

That doesn't lessen its impact as film or art, but it may give the next filmmaker who plans a $40,000,000 war epic a few second thoughts.

Poll.

ONE FROM THE HEART

January 20, 1982

Dazzling body, empty heart.

A Zoetrope Studio Production. Directed by Francis Coppola. Produced by Gray Frederickson and Fred Roos. Exec producer, Bernard Gersten; co-producer, Armyan Bernstein; screenplay, Bernstein, Coppola; story, Bernstein; features entire cast; camera (Metrocolor), Vittorio Storaro; director of photography, Ronald V. Garcia; editors, Arne Goursaud, Rudi Fehr, Randy Roberts; production design, Dean Tavoularis; special visual effects, Robert Swarthe; songs and music, Tom Waits; sung by Crystal Gayle and Tom Waits; art director, Angelo Graham; set decorators, Leslie McCarthy Frankenheimer, Gary Fettis; associate producer, Mona Skager. Reviewed at Radio City Music Hall. Jan. 15, 1982 (No MPAA rating). Running Time: 101 mins. (Color).

Hank	Frederic Forrest
Frannie	Teri Garr
Leila	Nastassia Kinski
Ray	Raul Julia
Maggie	Lainie Kazan
Moe	Harry Dean Stanton

As might have been expected, Francis Coppola's "One From The Heart" has emerged from its long, stormy production saga as another of the filmmaker's audacious ventures and a film hard to pigeonhole into any standard niche. Net result is a hybrid musical romantic fantasy, lavishing giddy heights of visual imagination and technical brilliance onto a wafer-thin story of true love turned sour, then sweet.

Its surrounding controversy and showmanship options aside, the film does emerge as something highly likeable, frequently funny, tuneful and occa-

sionally engaging. But for all its exciting visual dazzle and novel technological components, it's a curiously surface affair that for all its glitter tends to evaporate almost as quickly as it unfolds.

Paradoxically – considering its $27,000,000-area pricetag – the film ultimately comes across as a modst, amiable "small picture" that vastly overwhelms its tale and players through its sheer stylization. Its very originality and quirkiness pose an obvious commercial question mark. But careful selling and seeding – with Coppola's showmanship locomotive already steamed up – could well prompt some upbeat marketplace surprises. The film does have a shot at audience embrace.

Set against an intentionally artificial fantasy version of Las Vegas – with production designer Dean Tavoularis' studio-recreated casino strip, desert outposts and even the Vegas airport easily the film's best-paid and most dazzling stars – the film quite simply plots the break-up, separate dalliances and eventual happy ending of a pair of five-year lovers (Frederic Forrest and Teri Garr) over the course of a single Independence Day.

Bored with their humdrum mutual living and prompted by a major spat, they each walk into the Vegas evening to happen on chance romantic acquaintances that temporarily weave some magic and exoticism into their respective night apart. He meets a sultry, exotic circus girl (Nastassia Kinski) and knows underneath that it's all transitory; she's swept away by a suave Latino singing waiter (Raul Julia), intent on striking out into a new life of passion and exotic travel.

With cheerful intermittent turns by Harry Dean Stanton as Forrest's best friend and partner, and Lainie Kazan as Garr's blowsy sentimental barmaid buddy, the film's focus turns almost exclusively on Forrest's mounting efforts to win back Garr. The fairytale has an appropriately happy ending at fadeout.

As well-played as these principal characters are, their inherent one-dimensionality unfortunately puts emotional involvement in their travails at a premium. For most of the film their personal saga is too thoroughly overwhelmed by the grownup fantasyland landscapes that surround them and by the sheer neon-lit dazzle and breathtaking filmmaking technique and effects that highlight the venture.

Coppola, who cowrote the script with co-producer Armyan Bernstein from the latter's story, re-elevates the optical dissolve to new artistic heights as he charts their respective travels and overlapped yearnings. With the main narrative action unfolding in a seamless progression of long single takes, in which the camera weaves its ways with fluidity virtually unemcumbered by cuts, style becomes substance in every sense.

Underscoring and counterpointing the emotional tones is Tom Waits' bluesy-jazzy score and songs, with the composer and country balladeer Crystal Gayle warbling respective "boy" and "girl" roles. Apart from almost constant musical tracking, the narrative also gives way to a number of dance sequences (Julia and Garr cut a mean Latino rug) pedigreed in various Hollywood eras.

Painting this wonderland in some of the most stunningly atmospheric photography and magical lighting conceivable, the lensing achievement of Vittorio Storaro (who, per Coppola, was director of photography but lacks the 'director' credit – which goes to Ronald V. Garcia – because of union rules on offshore lensers) will be a hard act to follow in 1982. Particularly striking is the use of legerdemain [deceptive] lighting effects that transform day to night, exteriors to interiors with a mere wave of a wand. The film was shot in the onetime standard, near-square 1:33 image ratio, which Coppola intends to use wherever feasible

in the film's commercial playoff [run]. Net effect is quaint but seems hardly a rigorous requirement.

Obvious plaudits go to Robert Swarthe's special visual effects (lots of 'oohs and ahs' here, especially a nighttime fantasy sequence of a giant neon bulb billboard coming to life as Kinski dwarfing Forrest as she sings surrounded by kaleidoscopic light shows), and the editing of Arne Goursaud with Rudi Fehr and Randy Roberts.

Both tied to and apart from anything else, "One From The Heart" would seem to mark major technological breakthrough in its use of electronic video techniques throughout its entire pre-production phase. The apparent result is a sense of Coppola's utter control over every element in the complex canvas and a thoroughly fluid confidence in movement and effect.

Coppola has described this venture as the first stage in what promises to evolve into a further melding of video and film technique throughout an entire production. For now, the necessary next step would seem to be finding a strong enough narrative substance to live up to the stylistic and technological genius that can obviously surround it.

Step.

THE OUTSIDERS

March 23, 1983

Well-crafted but unexciting restless youth drama.

Hollywood, March 19. A Warner Bros. release. Produced by Fred Roos, Gray Frederickson. Directed by Francis Coppola. Features entire cast. Screenplay, Kathleen Knutsen Rowell, based on a novel by S.E. Hinton; camera (Technicolor, Panavision), Stephen H. Burum; editor, Anne Goursaud; music, Carmine Coppola; production design, Dean Tavoularis; set decoration, Gary Fettis; special visual effects, Robert Swarthe; costumes, Marge Bowers; sound design, Richard Beggs; sound (Dolby), Jim Webb; associate producer, Gian-Carlo Coppola; assistant director, David Valdes. Reviewed at the Pacific 4, Sherman Oaks, Calif., March 19, 1983. (MPAA Rating: PG). Running time: 91 mins. (Color).

Ponyboy Curtis	C. Thomas Howell
Dallas Winston	Matt Dillon
Johnny Cade	Ralph Macchio
Darrel Curtis	Patrick Swayze
Sodapop Curtis	Rob Lowe
Cherry Valance	Diane Lane
Two-Bit Matthews	Emilio Estevez
Steve Randle	Tom Cruise
Bob Sheldon	Leif Garrett
Tim Shephard	Glenn Withrow
Randy Anderson	Darren Dalton
Marcia	Michelle Meyrink
Jerry	Gailard Sartain
Buck Merrill	Tom Waits
Store Clerk	William Smith

Francis Coppola has made a well acted and crafted but highly conventional film out of S.E. Hinton's popular youth novel, "The Outsiders." Although set in the mid-1960s, pic feels very much like a 1950s drama about problem kids, such as those directed by Nicholas Ray and Elia Kazan, but is nowhere as penetrating or electric as the best work of those directors.

Warners is opening the film at 800 theatres nationwide and initial returns should be solid based on young people attraction to the material and good-looking thesps, as well as enduring interest in Coppola. But overall b.o. [box office] may only be modest, in line with pic's achievement.

Hinton wrote "The Outsiders," her first novel, while still at high school and since 1967 it has reportedly sold several million copies on the young adult circuit. Simple and direct in its humanization of small town "greasers" who are limited in education and feel like outcasts no matter what they do, tome takes a personal "us against the world" attitude which makes for easy teen identification.

Screenplay by Kathleen Knutsen Rowell is extremely faithful to the source material, even down to having the film open with the leading character and narrator, C. Thomas Howell, reciting the first lines of his literary effort while we see him writing them.

But as with such writers as Hemingway and Fitzgerald, dialog which reads naturally and evocatively on the page doesn't play as well on screen, and there's a decided difficulty of tone during the early sequences, as Howell and his buddies, Matt Dillon and Ralph Macchio horse around town, sneak into a drive-in and have an unpleasant confrontation with the Socs, rival gang from the well-heeled part of town.

When the Socs attack Howell and Macchio in the middle of the night, latter ends up killing a boy to save his friend, and the two flee to a hideaway in an abandoned rural church. Whole passage of their isolation reminds focibly of the Sal Mineo-James Dean relationship in "Rebel Without A Cause," and it is here that one of the most familiar themes of serious 1950s teen pics, that of "sensitive" youths trapped in a tough environment, comes to the fore.

It is also during the mid-section that the film starts coming to life, largely due to the integrity of the performances by Howell and Macchio. Younger, at about 16, and smaller than most of his cohorts, Howell is clearly a product of his deprived environment and upbringing (his parents died in an accident, leaving him and his two older brothers to fend for themselves), but also enjoys something of the budding intellectual's remove. He recites poetry, moons over the Socs' prettiest girl, Diane Lane, and makes it through the days on the lam [on the run] by reading "Gone With The Wind" (some visual effects of red-drenched sunsets backdropping the characters strongly evoke similar shots in "GWTW").

When the duo rescues some little kids from a fire in the church, they become the town's unlikely heroes. Macchio, however, is mortally injured in the blaze, and it just so happens that the Greasers and the Socs have scheduled an all-out rumble, in which Howell and Dillon participate with a "win one for Johnny" attitude.

Upon Macchio's death, Dillon, not his best friend Howell, freaks out, robs a store and is gunned down by the cops, while Howell is seen back at work on his tome.

It's all done with the utmost sincerity and, one might even say, reverence for the material, a feeling emphasized by Carmine Coppola's highly dramatic score, one which intensely evokes Leonard Rosenman's work on the James Dean pics "Rebel Without A Cause" and "East of Eden."

Although the kids in "Rebel" basically wanted to be understood and to feel part of society, a major difference with "The Outsiders" is that there is very little sense of rebellion. Nor are there any authority figures providing resistance to them. They're totally on their own, with marginal pasts and no definable futures, and the lack of concrete context for their behavior lessens the urgency of the tale as well as the fun often provided in such pics by cultural reference points.

Most satisfying elements remain the performances. Howell is truly impressive, a bulwark of relative stability in a sea of posturing and pretense. Macchio is also outstanding as his doomed friend, and Patrick Swayze is fine as the oldest brother forced into the role of parent. Only Dillon, star of the first Hinton film adaptation, "Tex," and the only b.o. [box office] name present, tends to overdo it, dragging on his cigarets with self conscious intensity and behaving in hyperkinetic fashion.

All craft work, notably Dean Tavoularis' production design and Stephen H. Burum's lensing, maintains the high standards expected in a Coppola film, but overall this seems at first viewing like the director's least personal and least ambitious pic in over a decade. Visually, film is characterized by heavy emphasis on the elements – fire, wind and water. Final impression is one of a respectable, but relatively unexciting, picture.

Cart.

RUMBLE FISH

October 12, 1983

Visually interesting but overwrought Coppola teen film.

Hollywood, Oct. 5. A Universal Picture release, produced by Fred Roos and Doug Claybourne. Directed by Francis Coppola. Features entire cast. Exec producer, Coppola. Screenplay, S.E. Hinton, Francis Coppola, based on Hinton's novel; camera (b&w), Stephen H. Burum; editor, Barry Malkin; sound, David Parker; production design, Dean Tavoularis; assistant director, David Valdes; music, Stewart Copeland. Reviewed at Universal Studios, L.A., Oct. 5, 1983. (MPAA Rating: R). Running time: 94 mins. (B&W/Color).

Rusty-James	Matt Dillon
Motorcycle Boy	Mickey Rourke
Patty	Diane Lane
Father	Dennis Hopper
Cassandra	Diana Scarwid
Steve	Vincent Spano
Smokey	Nicolas Cage
B.J.	Christopher Penn
Midget	Larry Fishburne
Patterson	William Smith

"Rumble Fish" is another Francis Coppola picture that's overwrought and over-thought with camera and characters that never quite come together in anything beyond consistently interesting. Like his other adaptation of an S.E. Hinton novel, "The Outsiders," it's probably looking at limited success.

Coppola is certainly too clever to fail at a project as simple as "Fish," but not wise enough to avoid the traps of teenage intellectualism he's trying to appeal to or encourage. Beautifully photographed in black and white by Stephen H. Burum, the picture really doesn't need all the excessive symbolism Coppola tries to cram into it.

For those who want it, however, "Fish" is another able examination of teenage alienation, centred around two brothers who are misfits in the ill-defined urban society they inhabit.

One, Matt Dillon, is a young tough inspired to no good purposes by an older brother, Mickey Rourke, once the toughest but now a bit of an addled eccentric, though remaining a hero to neighborhood thugs.

It's pretty clear from the start that Rourke has reached the end and it's only a question of how Dillon will turn out. But it's hard to care all that much, even if the issue were resolved, which it isn't.

Dillon and Rourke, though, turn in good performances as does Dennis Hopper as their drunken father and Diane Lane as Dillon's dumped-on girlfriend. Diana Scarwid is unfortunately underused as an addict hung up on Rourke. Nicolas Cage is a strong presence with a small part that's potentially more interesting than the brothers, but never pursued.

Title and a lot of the symbolism stem from Siamese fighting fish (photographed in color composite shots) which are unable to coexist with their fellows, or even an image of themselves. But as nature-film documentarians know, it's never a good idea to attribute human motives to wildlife behavior. And it can be equally dangerous to try the reverse.

Har.

THE COTTON CLUB

December 12, 1984

Uneven but still commercial Coppola spectacular.

An Orion Pictures release of a Zoetrope Studios production. Produced by Robert Evans. Executive producer, Dyson Lovell; coproducers, Silvio Tabet, Fred Roos; line producers, Barrie Osborne, Joseph Cusumano. Directed by Francis Coppola. Features entire cast. Screenplay, William Kennedy and Coppola, story by Kennedy, Coppola and Mario Puzo, suggested by a pictorial history by James Haskins. Camera (Technicolor), Stephen Goldblatt; editors, Barry Malkin, Robert Lovett; production designer, Richard Sylbert; costume design, Milena Canonero; principal choreographer, Michael Smuin; tap choreography, Henry LeTang; music, John Barry; musical recreations, Bob Wilber; sound mix (Dolby), Jack Jacobson. Reviewed at the Magno screening room, N.Y., Nov. 9, 1984. (MPAA Rating: R.) Running time: 127 mins. (Color).

Dixie Dwyer	Richard Gere
Sandman Williams	Gregory Hines
Vera Cicero	Diane Lane
Lila Rose Oliver	Lonette McKee
Owney Madden	Bob Hoskins
Dutch Schultz	James Remar
Vinent Dwyer	Nicolas Cage
Abbadabba Berman	Allen Garfield
Frenchy Demange	Fred Gwynne
Tish Dwyer	Gwen Verdon
Frances Flegenheimer	Lisa Jane Persky
Clay Williams	Maurice Hines
Sol Weinstein	Julian Beck
Madame St. Clair	Novella Nelson
Bumpy Rhodes	Larry Fishburne
Joe Flynn	John Ryan
Irving Stark	Tom Waits
Winnie Williams	Wynonna Smith
Sugar Coates	Charles (Honi) Coles
Cab Calloway	Larry Marshall
Lucky Luciano	Joe Dallesandro
Holmes	Woody Strode

The arrival of a new film by Francis Coppola brings with it the anticipation of greatness. His latest, "The Cotton Club," certainly isn't in the same league as his best pictures, but neither is it on the grim order of such recent efforts as "One From The Heart" and "Rumble Fish." For aficionados of the filmmaker, the latest effort may be a bit of a letdown, but it is by no means a disaster, nor is it a film lacking commercial appeal.

However, coming in at the reported $47,000,000, the '30s-era gangster saga set in the world of jazz music and dance will have a tough go at recouping its cost. Initial business should be quite brisk but the film's strongest point – its period music – is a doubtful long-term selling item for the prime moviegoing audience.

Comparisons are inevitable between the new film and Coppola's highly successful "Godfather" efforts. Initial hoopla played up the reteaming of the filmmaker with "Godfather" cronies, producer Robert Evans and scripter Mario Puzo (given a story credit here). However, it subsequently became apparent, through on-set and court tangles, that harmony did not reign supreme during production.

The new film certainly doesn't stint on ambition. Four stories thread through and intertwine in the picture. While the earlier Coppola gangster efforts had a firm hand on the balance between plot elements and characters, "The Cotton Club" emerges as uneven and sometimes unfocused and its tone giddily goes from the coldly realistic to frenzied fantasy.

Focus is on Dixie Dwyer (Richard Gere), a cornet player in a small Gotham club. As the film opens in 1928, Dixie interupts a solo to push a patron out of the way of a gunman's bullet. The thankful target turns out to be a racketeer, beer baron and nightclub owner Dutch Schultz (James Remar).

Schultz is soon throwing work Dixie's way and hires his brother, Vincent (Nicolas Cage), as a bodyguard. He also asks the musician to act as beard and escort his mistress Vera Cicero (Diane Lane), to various social functons. One such watering hole is the title Cotton Club owned by gangland peacemaker Owney Madden (Bob Hoskins) and operated by his right-hand man, Frenchie Demange (Fred Gwynne).

Final thread involves club tap star Sandman Williams (Gregory Hines) who partners with his brother Clay (Maurice Hines) and has his eyes and heart set on chorus girl Lila Rose Oliver (Lonette McKee). Also in the background are both the Dwyer and Williams' family matriarchs, Schultz' wife, business manager and enforcer, the Harlem-based club's real and fictional performers, guests and colorful underworld characters. It's a roster which virtually demands a detailed program.

Dramatically, Coppola and co-screenwriter William Kennedy, juggle a lot of balls in the air. The relationships between the two sets of brothers is a more obvious link between the various strands of the plot. However, in neither case does one come away feeling the potential emotional impact has been realized.

The Williams brothers become estranged as Sandman breaks away from the act to seek his own fortune. Later, having acquired notoriety, he returns to the club and half-heartedly joins Clay on stage when patrons demand a reunion. However, the emotion of the moment has the two unable to complete the tap routine and ending with a warm embrace.

The Dwyers go their separate ways as Dixie assumes a film career (Pioneer Pictures' "Mob Boss") and Vincent turns into a trigger-happy gunman. Acting as go-between, Dixie effects the exchange of ransom money, when his brother kidnaps Frenchie. Despite the awkwardness of the situation, Dixie tries to spirit his brother away but Vincent meets a violent end.

The parallel stories of Dixie and Sandman's professional rise prove more potent, thanks largely to a mixture of romance, music and gangland involvement. Hines and McKee generate real sparks in their relationship and latter adds an interesting dimension as light-skinned singer trying to hide her racial origins.

More complex, and less satisfying, is the hot-cold relationship between Dixie and Vera. Dixie's fear of Schultz and Vera's belief that the crime czar is her best ticket (he buys her a club) stall the prospects of a lasting union. However, as things heat up, Lane appears incapable of throwing off her cold exterior.

Highlights turly center with the gangsters' story and the many production numbers in the club. However, Coppola repeatedly frustrates one's appreciation of the musical elements by his continued cross-cutting to other action or truncating numbers. Not a single Cotton Club production is seen in its entirety.

Gere comes off well as both cypher and catalyst for the story. Any doubts about his ability to carry a picture can be dispelled with this film. And as an added bonus, he even does his own horn work. Also strong are Hines and McKee in the film's secondary story, but Lane is a genuine disappointment as Gere's love interest and as the ambitious singer (her voice dubbed once again) and club hostess tagging onto Schultz' coat tails.

Acting kudos go to Remar for a truly frightening portrait of the ruthless, erratic Schultz and to Hoskins and Gwynne who are a sheer delight whenever on screen. Gwynne's watch scene stands out as the film's best remembered non-musical moment and seems likely to earn Gwynne critical honors. Also of note are the Living Theatre's co-founder, Julian Beck, as a silent, sinister enforcer; the effervescent Gwen Verdon as Ma Dwyer and singer Tom Waits as the club's maitre'd.

Coppola and Kennedy have taken great pains to research the era and come up with an interesting mix of real and created characters of great authority. The effort somewhat resembles "Ragtime" but, aside from the historical basis of the material, one clearly sees the nods to both gangster and musical films of the 1930s, particularly those with the Warner Bros. brand attached.

Kennedy effects a real stamp on the film and one only regrets a feeling that the collaborators hurried into production without a script fixed in stone. Although great liberties are taken, there's a touch of George Raft in Dixie, Vera seems a variation on Texas Guinan, Lila could be the young Lena Horne and the Williams brother might have had their inspiration in the Nicholas brothers.

Technical work is generally first-rate with both sets and images providing an evocative rendering of the era. Original music by John Barry blends in nicely with Bob Wilber's reorchestrations of familiar period standards. Despite the fragments seen on screen, one can highly recommend choreographic efforts of Hines, Michael Smuin and Henry LeTang.

"The Cotton Club" serves up more entertainment highs than lows. Coppola's heart appears to be more in tune with the realistic elements of the story, so the fantasy finale comes as a bit of a shock. Still, so much good will have been served up in the picture that it's bound to pleased rather than irk audiences. The film should improve Coppola's personal stock and generate strong boxoffice returns even if it comes up short of being among the hallowed few topping the domestic theatrical gross figure of $100,000,000.

Klad.

PEGGY SUE GOT MARRIED

September 24, 1986

Smashing return to form by Francis Coppola. **A Tri-Star Pictures release from Rastar of a Tri-Star/Delphi IV and V Prods. production. Produced by Paul R. Gurian. Exective producer, Barrie M. Osborne. Directed by Francis Coppola. Stars Kathleen Turner. Screenplay, Jerry Leichtling, Arlene Sarner; camera (Deluxe color), Jordan Cronenweth; editor, Barry Malkin; music, John Barry; production design, Dean Tavoularis; art direction, Alex Tavoularis; set decoration, Marvin March; sound, Richard Bryce Goodman; costume design, Theadora Van Runkle; assistant director, Douglas Claybourne; casting, Pennie duPont. Reviewed at MGM Studios, Culver City, Calif. Sept 11, 1986. (MPAA Rating: PG-13.) Running time: 104 mins. (Color)**

Peggy Sue	Kathleen Turner
Charlie Bodell	Nicolas Cage
Richard Norvik	Barry Miller
Carol Heath	Catherine Hicks
Maddy Nagle	Joan Allen
Michael Fitzsimmons	Kevin J. O'Connor
Evelyn Kelcher	Barbara Harris
Jack Kelcher	Don Murray
Elizabeth Alvorg	Maureen O'Sullivan
Barney Alvorg	Leon Ames
Beth Bodell	Helen Hunt

Also with: Jim Carrey, Lisa Jane Persky, Lucinda Jenney, Wil Shriner, Sofia Coppola, John Carradine.

Hollywood – Who would have thought that Francis Coppola could make a sentimental, lighthearted adult version of "Back To The Future?" Well, he has and it's called "Peggie Sue Got Married." Film has the director's mark of distinction. It is provocative, well-acted, stylish and uneven. Pic is a marked improvement over anything else he's done lately and is sure to bring many disenchanted Coppola fans back to the theater.

"Peggy Sue" may seem to be a ripoff of "Back To The Future," but it was originally in production at the same time. When the pic was announced in October of 1984, Debra Winger was set to star and Penny Marshall to diret, but they left in a script dispute and the production was halted. The project was in limbo until Coppola took over last year with Kathleen Turner in the lead and the result is one terrific matchup.

Coppola doesn't overdirect Turner, a natural for playing Peggy Sue, the grown up all-American girl with a rebellious streak.

First-time scriptwriters Jerry Leichtling and Arlene Sarner have written a nice mix of sap and sass for Peggy Sue's character, a melancholy mother of two facing divorce who gets all dolled up in her 1950s-style ballgown to make a splash at her 25th high school reunion.

We get a clue that something special is going to happen to her just by the way cinematographer Jordan Cronenweth frames her face – backlit and dreamy-like – a technique he returns to at pivotal parts of the film.

Sure enough, she's selected Prom Queen. In all the excitement, she collapses on stage while accepting her crown – finding herself revived as an 18-year-old high school senior of the class of 1960.

Almost immediately, she realizes she's returned to her youth with all the knowledge and experience learned as an adult, quickly figuring out that she can alter the course of her future life by changing certain crucial decisions she made as a teenager.

Will she, or would we if we had to do it all again? This is a provocative question that is raised, and only superficially answered in "Peggy Sue."

The most important relationship for her is with steady boyfriend Charlie (Nicolas Cage), who she eventually marries, has two children by and only later seeks to divorce because of his infidelity.

Cage is almost a caricature of the primping, self-centred, immature high school jerk who is really insecure deep down. His character becomes exaggerated as the film progresses, giving a good clue to his future notoriety as an obnoxious tv appliance pitchman. He is strangely unintelligible at times but the dialog isn't missed.

Turner seems so in control of her feelings throughout most of the film and he remains fairly static, which leaves one wondering why, with all her new found perspective, she goes for him all over again.

Film stereotypifies the other people important in her teenage years (adoring parents, wise grandparents, gawky sister), but it does heighten the amusement factor when their one-dimensional personalities are played off against hers.

What makes this treatment unique is that the jokes aren't so much derivative of pop culture, as they were in "Back To The Future," but are instead found in the learned wisdom of a middle-aged woman reacting to her own teenage dilemmas.

At one point, she makes a play for the outcast beatnik Michael Fitzsimmons (Kevin J. O'Connor), who she always believed to be a lot more sensitive and sexy than her boyfriend. O'Connor plays the part to the hilt – taking her to some moonlit area when he very seriously recites some of his drekky poetry. It's a hoot.

Film also manages to tug on the old heartstrings without being maudlin as Turner revisits with her parents (Barbara Harris, Don Murray) and grandparents (Maureen O'Sullivan, Leon Ames), realizing she's taken them for granted and now has a chance to make up for past ingratitudes.

Sometimes Coppola doesn't know how to end his pics, and "Peggy Sue" is another example. Contrived scene at the men-only club is silly and breaks the flow of the film.

Tech credits, as in all of Coppola's efforts, are terrific.

Soundtrack os 1950s tunes, including the Buddy Holly classic from which the film's title is taken, are integrated well into the story.

Brit.

GARDENS OF STONE

May 6, 1987

Disappointing Vietnam home front drama. **A Tri-Star Pictures release from Tri-Star-ML Delphi Premier Prods. Produced by Michael I. Levy, Francis Coppola. Executive producers, Stan Weston, Jay Emmett, Fred Roos. Co-executive producer, David Valdes. Directed by Coppola. Screenplay, Ronald Bass, based on novel by Nicholas Proffitt; camera (Deluxe color), Jordan Cronenweth; editor, Barry Malkin; music, Carmine Coppola; production design, Dean Tavoularis; art direction, Alex Tavoularis; set decoration, Gary Fettis; sound (Dolby stereo), Thomas Causey; costumes, Willa Kim, Judianna Makovsky; assistant director, David Valdes; casting, Janet Hirshenson, Jane Jenkins, Bonnie Timmermann. Reviewed at Lorimar screening room, L.A., April 24, 1987. (MPAA Rating: R.) Running time: 111 mins. (Color)**

Clell Hazard	James Caan
Samantha Davis	Anjelica Huston
"Goody" Nelson	James Earl Jones
Jackie Willow	D.B. Sweeney
Homer Thomas	Dean Stockwell
Rachel Field	Mary Stuart Masterson
Slasher Williams	Dick Anthony Williams
Betty Rae	Lonette McKee
Lt. Weber	Sam Bottoms
Pete Deveber	Elias Koteas
Flanagan	Larry Fishburne
Wildman	Casey Siemaszko
Also with: Peter Masterson, Carlin Glynn, Erik Holland, Bill Graham.	

Hollywood – "Gardens of Stone," Francis Coppola's muddled meditation on the Vietnam War, seems to take its name not so much from the Arlington Memorial

Cemetery, where much of the action takes place, but from the stiffness of the characters its portrays. As story telling, it is a seriously flawed film. As a political tract, it is shamelessly incomplete. And as film-making, it is a major disappointment.

Coppola's name above the title will ensure some interest at the box-office, but somber tone and turgid pace are sure to keep the lines short.

Structured around the small details and formal rituals of military life, pic opens and closes with a funeral and in between is supposed to be the emotional stuff that makes an audience care about the death of a soldier. But it is a case of form substituting for feeling and although there is unlikely to be a dry eye in the house at the finale, there is a hollowness at the film's core.

As a two-time combat vet biding his time training young recruits for the Old Guard, the Army's ceremonial unit at Fort Myer, Va., Clell Hazard (James Caan) knows the war is wrong but cannot oppose it. Rather than protest, he feels it is his responsibility to prepare the young soldiers as best he can, especially young Private Willow (D.B. Sweeney), the son of an old Korean war buddy.

Script by Ronald Bass, from Nicholas Proffitt's novel, attempts to create sympathetic soldiers whose first loyalty is to their brothers in arms. It's a point of view, however, that totally begs the issue of moral responsibility and seals the soldiers off from the rest of the world.

Indeed it is a world unto itself as Caan swaps tales of horror and heroism with his buddy "Goody" Nelson (James Earl Jones). It is hard to grasp the affection and values of these men although they are given numerous opportunities to hold forth. Since there is little of no organic flow to the action, scenes are often merely set-ups for awkward exposition.

Most contrived of the relationships is Caan's affair with Anjelica Huston who plays a Washington Post reporter vehemently opposed to the war. For starters the attraction is assumed rather than demonstrated and Huston seems far too intelligent to make the choice she does. Basically the supportive woman waiting in the wings, she also has enough stilted dialog to destroy her character.

At the heart of the film is Caan's connection to the youngster, but Sweeney's character is such a gung-ho soldier that even the explanations offered here can't condone his actions. On a more visceral level, he's simply not an engaging presence.

Staging is surprisingly static and Coppola's view of army life lacks the emotional underpinnings to allow an audience to embrace its apologist politics. It is not enough to simply feel strongly about a position to make it dramatically convincing.

More to the point and Coppola's proven strengths are some lovely ensemble scenes such as when Sweeney courts his wife-to-be (Mary Stuart Masterson) and gets a decidedly mixed reception from her family (played by her real-life parents, Peter Masterson and Carlin Glynn). Here the cross-fire and play of conflicting values creates a tension that says more about the era than the puffed up posturing of the rest of the film.

Given the material they have to work with, performances fail to ignite the characters with Caan having his moments but overall remaining mostly an enigma. Huston is often stiff and stagey while Jones is in another universe all together.

As in most Coppola films, production values are first-rate with longtime collaborator Dean Tavoularis' production design evoking the mood of the times. Jordan Cronenweth's cinematography is dark and suggestive, if only the film had more to say.

Jagr.

TUCKER: THE MAN AND HIS DREAM

August 3, 1988

A Paramount Pictures release of a Lucasfilm Ltd. production from Zoetrope Studios. Produced by Fred Roos, Fred Fuchs. Executive producer, George Lucas. Directed by Francis Ford Coppola. Screenplay, Arnold Schulman, David Seidler; camera (Technovision, Technicolor), Vittorio Storaro; editor, Priscilla Nedd; music, Joe Jackson; additional music, Carmine Coppola; sound (Dolby), Michael Evje; production design, Dean Tavoularis; art direction, Alex Tavoularis; set design, Bob Goldstein, Jim Pohl; set decoration, Armin Ganz; costume design, Milena Canonero; sound design, Richard Beggs; associate producer, Teri Fettis; assistant director, H. Gordon Boos; stunt coordinator-second unit director, Buddy Joe Hooker; casting, Janet Hirshenson, Jane Jenkins. Reviewed at Paramount Studios, L.A., July 29, 1988. MPAA Rating: PG. Running time: 111 mins.

Preston Tucker	Jeff Bridges
Vera Tucker	Joan Allen
Abe Karatz	Martin Landau
Eddie Dean	Frederic Forrest
Jimmy Sakuyama	Mako
Howard Hughes	Dean Stockwell
Sen. Homer Ferguson	Lloyd Bridges
Alex Tremulis	Elias Koteas
Marilyn Lee Tucker	Nina Siemaszko
Preston Tucker Jr	Christian Slater
Noble Tucker	Corky Nemec
Johnny Tucker	Anders Johnson
Frank	Marshall Bell
Stan	Don Novello
Kirby	Jay O. Sanders
Kerner	Peter Donat
Bennington	Dean Goodman
Millie	Patti Austin

Hollywood – The true story of a great American visionary who was thwarted, if not destroyed, by the established order, "Tucker: The Man And His Dream" represents the sunniest imaginable telling of an at least partly tragic episode in recent history.

Like a glittering, briskly moving big brass band, splashy film parades the life of revolutionary automobile designer Preston Tucker across the screen so as to make it resemble a noisy, colorful, rambunctious public spectacle. Approach leaves little room for depth, emotion or a rewarding human dimension, but the upbeat tempo and attitude carry the viewer right along through an irresistably engaging tale, one that should activate a fair measure of interest at the boxoffice.

Francis Ford Coppola is on record to the effect that this "Tucker" is considerably different, less bitter and more optimistic, than the film he originally envisioned years ago, and one only has to recall the dark, brooding qualities of the "Godfather" epics and "Apocalypse Now" to imagine what "Tucker" might have been like had the director tackled it back in the 1970s.

Film that has emerged represents the first artistic collaboration between Coppola and George Lucas, with one of the them as director, since the similarly car-obsessed "American Graffiti" in 1973, and one might confidently guess that Lucas had more than a little to do with determining the rosy, positive attitude toward life's vicissitudes on view here.

On the other hand, Tucker's life and career present so many parallels to Coppola's own it is easy to see why he has coveted this project for so long. Industryites will nod in recognition of this story of a self-styled genius up against business interests hostile to his innovative ideas, but also will note the accepting, unbelligerent stance adopted toward the terms of the stuggle.

In the mild echo of "Citizen Kane," this exquisitely produced picture opens with a facsimile of an in-house promotional film about Tucker's activities up through World War II, showing how his speedy combat vehicle proved impractical for the Army but how his design for machine-gun turrets won wide acceptance.

After World War II, seemingly on the strength of his enthusiasm alone, Tucker got a small core of collaborators to work on his dream project, which he called "the first completely new car in 50 years" and was sold as "The car of tomorrow – today." Boasting a striking. streamlined look, the Tucker promised such advanced features as a rear engine, disc breakes, fuel injection, a center headlight, seat belts and a pop-out windshield, and would sell for less than $2,500.

With a factory in Chicago, Tucker managed to turn out 50 of his beauties, but vested interests in Detroit and Washington dragged him into court on fraud charges, shutting him down and effectively ending his automobile career. As his moneyman tells him, "You build the car too good."

It's a classically American tale of the maverick trying to buck the system, and Coppola presents it all as if his stage were a 3-ring circus, a place where introspection, analysis and second thoughts are not allowed. Rare is the scene with only two people in it, and Coppola does give a strong impression of what it's like to create something ambitious under enormous private pressure and public scrutiny.

Everything about Coppola's bright rendition of Arnold Schulman and David Seidler's peppy script expresses a winning, can-do attitude, and the pros and cons of this approach are perfectly exemplified in Jeff Bridges' performance in the leading role. Flashing his charming smile and oozing cocky confidence, his Tucker is inspiring because he won't be depressed or defeated by anything. At the same time, however, the viewer can't claim to know him at all, for nothing resembling a 3-dimensional human being ever emerges.

In fact, virtually everyone in the film makes a vivid, appealing impression, but is restricted similarly by the 1-note, let's-put-on-a-show angle. However, Martin Landau manages to break through with a highly sympathetic, sometimes moving portrayal of Tucker's financial manager, and Dean Stockwell, as Howard Hughes, effectively presides over an eerie scene, brilliantly staged in the Spruce Goose hangar, in which two iconoclastic, beleaguered industrialists briefly meet.

Technically, the film is a dream. Shooting in the San Francisco Bay Area, production designer Dean Tavoularis, costume designer Milena Canonero and cinematographer Vittorio Storaro have conjured up a splashy, slightly stylized vision of the late 1940s that bears some resemblance to magazine photography of the period. Score by pop music figure Joe Jackson consists of propulsively uptempo big band material. And then there are the cars themselves, a constant pleasure to behold.

Rousing approach to Tucker's life here takes the view that it was the man's dreams, and his inspiring attempt to make them come true, that remain important, not the fact that he lost when the final buzzer sounded. This may make the picture more accessible to the general public than it might have been otherwise, but it also flattens out the ironies, complexities and richness inherent in the story itself.

Cart.

NEW YORK STORIES

March 1–7, 1989

Hollywood. A Buena Vista release of a Touchstone presentation of a Jack Rollins and Charles H. Joffe production. Film in three episodes, produced by Robert Greenhut.

Life Lessons

Produced by Barbara DeFina. Directed by Martin Scorsese. Screenplay, Richard Price; camera (Duart color; Metrocolor prints), Nestor Almendros; editor, Thelma Schoonmaker; production design, Kristi Zea; art direction, Wray Steven Graham; set decoration, Nina F. Ramsey; costume design, John Dunn; sound, James Sabat; assistant director, Joseph Reidy; casting, Ellen Lewis.

Lionel Dobie	Nick Nolte
Paulette	Rosanna Arquette
Phillip Fowler	Patrick O'Neal
Reuben Toro	Jesse Borrego
Gregory Stark	Steve Buscemi
Peter Gabriel	Himself
Paulette's Friend	Illeana Douglas

Life Without Zoe

Produced by Fred Roos, Fred Fuchs. Directed by Francis Coppola. Screenplay, Francis Coppola, Sofia Coppola; camera (color), Vittorio Storaro; editor, Barry Malkin; music, Carmine Coppola, Kid Creole and the Coconuts; production design, Dean Tavoularis; art direction, Speed Hopkins; set decoration, George DeTitta Jr.; costume design, Sofia Coppola; sound, James Sabat; assistant director, Joseph Reidy; casting, Aleta Chapelle.

Zoe	Heather McComb
Charlotte	Talia Shire
Claudio	Giancarlo Giannini
Clifford, The Doorman	Paul Herman
Jimmy	James Keane
Hector	Don Novello
Abu	Selim Tlili
Street Musician	Carmine Coppola
Princess Soroya	Carole Bouquet

Oedipus Wrecks

Produced by Robert Greenhut. Executive producers, Jack Rollins, Charles H. Joffe. Written and directed by Woody Allen. Camera (colour), Sven Nykvist; editor, Susan E. Morse; production design, Santo Loquasto; art direction, Speed Hopkins; set decoration, Susan Bode; costume design, Jeffrey Kurland; sound, James Sabat; assistant director, Thomas Reilly; casting, Juliet Taylor. Reviewed at the Walt Disney Studios, Burbank, Calif., Feb. 22, 1989. MPAA Rating: PG. Running time: 123 mins.

Sheldon Mills	Woody Allen
Lisa	Mia Farrow
Treva	Julie Kavner
Mother	Mae Questel
Psychiatrist	Marvin Chatinover
Aunt Ceil	Jessie Keosian
Shandu, The Magician	George Schindler
Rita	Bridgit Ryan
Mayor Edward I. Koch	Himself

'New York Stories' showcases the talents of three of the modern American cinema's foremost auteurs, Martin Scorsese, Francis Coppola and Woody Allen. As seems always to be the case with multi-episode projects, not all the segments turn out well, and the ratio here is two winners to one clinker.

Picture will obviously draw a limited

buff crowd automatically interested in the directors, but prospects beyond that look dicey because each installment is pitched to a different audience. Scorsese's is aimed at serious-minded adults, Coppola's to children, and Allen's to a more general public looking for laughs. Making this into a commercial success would represent a true victory for Disney.

Filmmakers were given carte blanche to develop subjects that dealt in some way with life in Gotham and might not fit a normal running time. With just a couple of exceptions, they reassembled top collaborators from previous pictures, and main thing works have in common is their setting among different segments of New York's privileged, elite class.

Scorsese's "Life Lessons" gets things off to a pulsating start, as Nestor Almendros' camera darts, swoops and circles around Nick Nolte and Rosanna Arquette as they face the end of an intense romantic entanglement. Looking not unlike his parasitic hobo of "Down And Out In Beverly Hills," the leonine Nolte plays a leading light of the downtown art scene, an abstract painter unprepared for a major gallery opening three weeks away.

Announcing that she's had a fling, Arquette, Nolte's lover and artistic protege, agrees to stay on in his loft as long as she no longer has to sleep with him but doesn't make life easy for him, as she's continually creating a scene and even brings a pickup back to their bed for a night.

Through all the domestic adversity, the agitated Nolte, to the accompaniment of Procol Harum's "Whiter Shade of Pale," Dylan's "Like a Rolling Stone" and a host of other tunes, furiously works on his enormous canvases.

Sometimes conjuring up memories of his first film, "Who's That Knocking At My Door?," Scorsese cogently works out his theme of how art can thrive on emotional turmoil. While one can wonder at Nolte so

patiently tolerating Arquette's tantrums and abuse, it becomes clear that he actually needs it to egg him on in his work.

Working from a deft script by Richard Price, who penned "The Color of Money," for him, Scorsese and his team use every camera, editing, optical, music and sound effects trick in the book to make this a dynamic display of almost off-hand mastery.

Nolte is at his most appealing here, and sidetrips out of the loft provide a voyeuristic tour of the club, gallery and bar scene, with such in-crowd types as performance artist Steve Buscemi, Peter Gabriel, Deborah Harry, Price and Scorsese himself putting in brief appearances. At 45 minutes, this is the longest of the episodes.

At 33 minutes, Francis Coppola's "Life Without Zoe" is the shortest of the three, but that is still not nearly short enough, as the director and his daughter Sofia have concocted the flimsiest of conceits for their contribution.

Vignette is a wispy urban fairytale about a 12-year-old girl who, because her parents are on the road most of the time, basically lives alone at the ritzy Sherry Netherland Hotel while attending a private school populated by kids of some of the world's richest people.

This milieu of privileged children is a fresh one with plenty of potential in numerous directions, and during the course of the pretty, fanciful nothingness that occupies the half-hour, the mind wanders to what might have been.

On the one hand, Coppola, himself a resident of the Sherry Netherland, could have made a very personal film about his own family's life in such a rarified environment. Alternatively, the offspring of diplomats, Arab Sheiks and world famous artists throwing elaborate parties and prematurely assuming the airs of their parents provides plenty of material for delicious satire.

As it stands, this whimsy goes nowhere, as little Zoe floats through the lush wonderland of production designer

Dean Tavoularis and lenser Vittorio Storaro on her way to a preposterous reunion with her folks in front of the Parthenon. Given the chance to say anything he wanted, it comes as a staggering disappointment that Coppola chose to say nothing, or worse, had nothing on his mind.

Happily, Woody Allen salvages matters rather nicely with "Oedipus Wrecks." As soon as he commences complaining about his mother to his psychiatrist, the viewer breathes a welcome sigh of relief that Allen, absent as an actor from the screen since "Hannah And Her Sisters" three years ago, is back with jokes up his sleeve.

As the title suggests, subject here is the Jewish mother syndrome, of which Allen moans he is still a victim at age 50. When Allen takes shiksa girlfriend Mia Farrow home for dinner, he winces as Mama assails him for choosing a blond with three kids.

In a hilarious sequence, Allen's fondest wish – that his mother just disappear – comes true when a magician literally loses her in the course of a trick. To relate the upshot of his would spoil the fun, but Allen comes to suffer the ultimate in mother domination via a conception that calls to mind the rampaging giant beast of "Everything You Always Wanted to Know About Sex."

Much of the humor is of the Catskills circuit variety, and while several of the jokes detonate belly laughs, others are admittedly on the feeble side. About five minutes could profitably have been shaved from the 40-minute running time, and there are those who will assert that this simply represents a vehicle for Allen's uncomfortable squirming about his own Jewishness. In this vein, "Oedipus" marks the first time Allen has ended up with a Jewish woman since the earliest days of his screen career.

Pic concludes with five minutes of credits, certainly the longest end credit roll since "Who Framed Roger Rabbit."

Cart.

THE GODFATHER, PART III

December 17, 1990

A Paramount release from Zoetrope Studios. Produced and directed by Francis Ford Coppola. Executive producers, Fred Fuchs, Nicholas Gage. Screenplay, Mario Puzo, Coppola. Camera (Technicolor), Gordon Willis; editor, Barry Malkin, Lisa Fruchtman, Walter Murch; music, Carmine Coppola; additional music and themes, Nino Rota; sound (Dolby), Clive Winter; sound design, Richard Beggs; production design, Dean Tavoularis; supervising art director, Alex Tavoularis; set design (Italy), Mario Teresa Barbasso, Nazzareno Piana; supervising set decorator, Gary Fettis; set decorator (Italy), Franco Fumagalli; costume design, Milena Canonero; associate producer, Marina Gefter; coproducers, Fred Roos, Gray Frederickson, Charles Mulvehill; assistant directors, H. Gordon Boos, Gianni Arduini-Plaisant (Italy); casting, Janet Hirshenson, Jane Jenkins, Roger Mussenden. Reviewed at the Loews Astor Plaza, N.Y., Dec. 12, 1990. MPAA Rating: R. Running time: 161 mins.

Michael Corleone	Al Pacino
Kay Adams	Diane Keaton
Connie Corleone Rizzi	Talia Shire
Vincent Mancini	Andy Garcia
Don Altobello	Eli Wallach
Joey Zasa	Joe Mantegna
B.J. Harrison	George Hamilton
Grace Hamilton	Bridget Fonda
Mary Corleone	Sofia Coppola
Cardinal Lamberto	Raf Vallone
Anthony Corleone	Franc D'Ambrosio
Archbishop Gilday	Donal Donnelly
Al Neri	Richard Bright
Frederick Keinszig	Helmut Berger
Dominic Abbandando	Don Novello

Also with: John Savage, Franci Citti, Mario Donatone, Vittorio Duse, Enzo Robutti, Michele Russo, Al Martino, Robert Cicchini, Rogerio Miranda.

Faced with the extraordinary task of recapturing magic he created 16 and 18 years ago, Francis Ford Coppola has come very close to completely succeeding with "The Godfather Part III."

While certain flaws may prevent it from being regarded as the full equal of its predecessors, which are generally ranked among the greatest modern Amercan films, it nonetheless matches them in narrative intensity, epic scope, sociopolitical analysis, physical beauty and deep feeling for its characters and milieu. In addition, it is certainly the most personal of the three for the director.

It is impossible to know if Paramount's $55 million-plus production investment will yield huge profits, but it should stand as a major b.o. [box office] attraction.

Dragged back into bloody gangland activities after laboriously enshrouding himself in the trappings of respectability, Al Pacino's Michael Corleone laments, "Just when I thought I was out, they pull me back in." This could be read as Coppola's comment upon his own involvement in this celebrated trilogy.

Once again, Coppola has managed to fuse matters of close concern to him with the stuff of richly satisfying commercial entertainment. Preoccupations with aging, diminished power, family, passing the mantle, sin and redemption are easily combined with dramatic familial and political intrigue, violent power plays, international high finance and corruption in the Vatican. Most of it plays beautifully.

Reminders of the earlier pictures are present both explicitly, via brief clips, and implicity, through the repetition of story-telling motifs. Like the original, Part III

opens with a lengthy festival celebration punctuated by backroom dealings. It is 1979, and Michael Corleone, having divested himself of his illegal operations, is being honored by the Catholic Church for his abundant charitable activities.

The party at the family's lavish New York apartment introduces characters both familiar and new. Michael's ex-wife Kay (Diane Keaton), now remarried, comes to see him for the first time in eight years, principally to support the desire of the couple's son Anthony (Franc D'Ambrosio) to quit law school and become an opera singer. Unmarried and without a romantic attachment, Michael receives his emotional support from his sister Connie (Talia Shire).

Hopeful of bringing his family closer together, Michael dotes on his daughter Mary (Sofia Coppola), and understandably becomes perturbed by her affair with her cousin Vincent (Andy Garcia), hot-headed, violence-prone illegitimate son of Michael's late brother Sonny, Vincent has been unhappily working for slumlord and old-style thug Joey Zasa (Joe Mantegna), who has taken on Michael's less savory holdings.

Also on the scene are friendly rival Don Altobello (Eli Wallach), new counsel B.J. Harrison (George Hamilton), replacing the absent Robert Duvall's Tom Hagen, Hagen's priest son Andrew (John Savage), singer Johnny Fontane (Al Martino), the highly place Archbishop Gilday (Donal Donnelly) and a journalist (Bridget Fonda) who seeks an interview with Don Corleone but happily settles for a roll in the hay with Vincent.

Bad blood between the ruthless Zasa and the Corleone family mounts just as Michael tries, with $600 million, to buy a controlling interest in the European conglomerate Immobiliare, a move that would cement his business legitimacy and financial future. The company is owned by venerable European families presented as being even more corrupt than the Mafia, and both sides lobby for the favor of the Vatican, which must ratify the Corleone takeover.

But old ways die hard, as Zasa, feeling slighted, spectacularly massacres most of the old dons at an Atlantic City conclave. Michael and Altobello escape with their lives, whereupon the irrepressible Vincent undertakes a personal vendetta against his impudent former boss.

After exactly midpoint, 80 minutes, the action switches to Italy, where it remains for the duration. Ostensibly, the family is gathering in Sicily to attend the operatic debut of Anthony, but there is much business to look after. Pacino and Wallach's old dons can't help begin scheming against one another, much as they profess to want to live out their remaining days quietly.

In one extremely potent scene, Michael begins confessing his countless sins to a cardinal (Raf Vallone), which forces him to confront his most heinous crime, the murder of his brother Fredo. Even more powerful is the sequence in which Michael officially anoints his bastard nephew as a Corleone, giving him the power of a don.

But the best is still yet to come. In one of the most masterful examples of sustained intercutting in cinema, Anthony's performance on opening night in "Cavalleria Rusticana" serves as the backdrop for several murderous missions.

Both Michael and Altobello are targets at the opera house, two financial kingpins are victimized, a bishop is pursued and the Pope himself (the actual John Paul I, who died mysteriously after a very short reign) falls under an assassin's hand. Suspense generated here is genuine and considerable, and is topped off by a rather shocking denouement that, given the death of one of Coppola's sons a few years ago, could not be more deeply felt.

With one glaring exception, which may unfortunately become the subject of an inordinate amount of criticism, casting and acting is exemplary down the line. For the third time out in his career role, Pacino is magnificent. With his character trying to take the initiative in reconciling his family and pushing through new business deals, Pacino is more animated and varied than he was going into his deep freeze in Part II. He manages to generate considerable sympathy despite his venal history, and injects a measure of rueful humor as well.

Andy Garcia brings much-needed youth and juice to the ballsy Vincent, heir apparent to the Corleone tradition, much as James Caan sparked the first film and Robert De Niro invigorated the second.

Looking and acting better than she has before as Kay (hardly her most memorable role), Diane Keaton proves a welcome, if brief, presence in warming the film, and Talia Shire seems pleased with the opportunity to do some dirty work at long last. Wallach, Mantegna, Vallone, Donnelly and Fonda are all impressive, while Hamilton has very little to do but stand behind Pacino.

Film's main flaw, unavoidably, is Sofia Coppola in the important, but not critical, role of Michael's daughter. Ungainly, afflicted with a valley girl accent and not an actress who can hold her own in this august company, the director's daughter simply doesn't cut it. This renders pic's main romantic element uncompelling and essentially unbelievable, and undercuts the force of the ending.

Unfortunate casting decision was made after original actress Winona Ryder had to bow out at the start of production and created a furor within the company. Sad to say, the naysayers were correct.

A few awkward lines of dialog pop up here and there, and finale feels too abrupt, as Coppola seems to put too quick a capper on his great saga. But these are the only notable drawbacks in a mostly outstanding work.

As before, production values are spectacular. Myriad settings created by Dean Tavoularis and countless costumes fashioned by Milena Canonero provide a constant visual delight. Gordon Willis' cinematography, dark as before, gloriously matches his supreme accomplishments on the preceding films.

Carmine Coppola's score artfully incorporates the late Nino Rota's themes into outstanding new musical backgrounding, and editing by Barry Malkin, Lisa Fruchtman and Walter Murch keeps the disparate elements in balance while shining in individual setpieces.

Like Michael Corleone, Coppola seems to have been looking for a certain absolution with this film and, in exploring his major themes here so richly, with the maturity and resignation gained with age, he has arguably achieved it.

He has also created a dramatic and commercial powerhouse that can stand easily on its own and as the conclusion of a remarkable trilogy.

Cart.

BRAM STOKER'S DRACULA

November 9 1992

A Columbia release of an American Zoetrope/Osiris Films production. Produced by Francis Ford Coppola, Fred Fuchs, Charles Mulvehill. Executive producers, Michael Apted, Robert O'Connor. Directed by Coppola. Screenplay, Hart, based on Stoker's novel. Camera (Technicolor), Michael Ballhaus; editors, Nicholas C. Smith, Glen Scantlebury, Anne Goursaud; music, Wojciech Kilar; production design, Thomas Sanders; art direction, Andrew Precht; set decoration, Garrett Lewis; costume design, Eiko Ishioka; sound (Dolby), Robert Janiger; sound design, Leslie Shatz; visual effects-2nd unit director, Roman Coppola; special visual effects, Fantasy II Film Effects; makeup-hair design, Michele Burke; special makeup effects, Greg Cannom; associate producer, Susie Landau; assistant director, Peter Giuliano; 2nd unit camera, Steve Yaconelli; co-producers, James V. Hart, John Veitch; casting, Victoria Thomas. Reviewed at Ziegfeld Theater, N.Y., Oct. 30, 1992. MPAA Rating: R. Running time: 123 mins.

Dracula	Gary Oldman
Mina/Elisabeta	Winona Ryder
Van Helsing	Anthony Hopkins
Jonathan Harker	Keanu Reeves
Dr. Jack Seward	Richard E. Grant
Lord Arthur Holmwood	Cary Elwes
Quincey P. Morris	Bill Campbell
Lucy Westenra	Sadie Frost
R.M. Renfield	Tom Waits

Also with: Monica Bellucci, Michaela Bercu, Florina Kendrick, Jay Robinson.

Francis Ford Coppola's take on the Dracula legend is a bloody visual feast. Both the most extravagant screen telling of the oft-filmed story and the one most faithful to its literary source, this rendition sets grand romantic goals for itself that aren't fulfilled emotionally, and it is gory without being at all scary.

Grandiose production's main pleasures reside in its exceptional design and in seeing the original tale told in full. The Dracula name, such as it is, and a mighty promo push for its Friday the 13th bow should generate some strong early frame numbers, but pic's extreme adult nature will limit potential with younger auds [audiences], and reaction will be mixed.

Bram Stoker finally achieves title card billing à la Jackie Collins and Danielle Steele as James V. Hart is the first screenwriter with the good idea to fundamentally follow the wonderful 1897 novel. The considerably different 1927 Hamilton Deane-John Balderston stage play yielded the best known Dracula films, notably the 1931 Bela Lugosi version.

Hart sets epic parameters for his script with a prologue introducing Dracula's historical origins as Vlad the Impaler, a 15th century Romanian king who fought off Turkish invaders. As dramatically sketched here, the ruler's inamorata, Elisabeta, killed herself upon receiving false news of his death in battle, whereupon the monarch furiously renounced God and began his centuries-long devotion to evil.

In casting Winona Ryder as both Elisabeta and Mina Murray, the overarching story becomes Dracula's quest for recapturing his great love. Unfortunately, familiar plotting, Coppola's coldly magisterial style and Gary Oldman's plain appearance in the title role combine to prevent this strategy from working in more than theory.

But it does set a serious tone, and the director manages to steer a relatively steady course embracing dramatic convic-

tion as well as the humor necessary to send up the vampire conventions that have inevitably become hoary with constant use. He also invests it with a primal sexuality and animalism consistent with the book.

Sent to the count's Transylvanian castle to advise him on London real estate, Jonathan Harker (Keanu Reeves) ends up being held prisoner there and being feasted upon by his host's three luscious concubines. Dracula, meanwhile, is plotting his unique conquest of Britain, which involves transporting coffins filled with fertile Transylvanian earth and infecting the populace via incarnations as wolf, bat and fog.

Mina awaits the return of her fiancé Harker in the company of her best friend, Lucy (Sadie Frost), a popular young lady whom Dracula soon seduces into the world of the undead. In a desperate bid to save her life, a beau, Dr. Jack Seward (Richard E. Grant), calls upon the eminent Dutch doctor/metaphysician Abraham Van Helsing (Anthony Hopkins), and they, along with Lucy's fiancé Lord Arthur Holmwood (Cary Elwes) and footloose Yank Quincey Morris (Bill Campbell) team to foil Dracula as he sets his sights on Mina.

Shot almost entirely on sound-stages, film has the fee of an old-fashioned, 1930s, studio-enclosed production made with the benefit of '90s technology. From the striking, blood-drenched prologue on, viewer is constantly made aware of cinema artiface in its grandest manifestations.

Thomas Sanders' production design, Michael Ballhaus' lensing, Michele Burke's makeup and especially Eiko Ishioka's amazing costumes create a dark world of heightened irreality within a context both Gothic and Victorian. Linking all these elements together are many exceptional transitions – dissolves, superimpositions, juxtapositions and cuts that have been worked out with tremendous premeditation and imagination. Visual effects and second unit director Roman Coppola no doubt had a hand in all this, along with the three editors, and the threateningly turbulent score by Wojciech Kilar furthers the brooding mood.

Using a Romanian accent, Oldman comes up with a few unintelligible line readings, but enacts Dracula with wit, sophistication and proper seriousness. The problem may be, however, that the fundamentally fine young character actor and chameleon lacks the charisma and insinuating personality that would put across Coppola's conception of a highly sexualized vampire.

Other performances range from a bit stiff (the young male contingent) to playfully energetic (Hopkins) to compelling (Tom Waits as the insect-eating lunatic Renfield). Ryder has just the right combination of intelligence and enticing looks as Mina.

Coppola doesn't push it, but underlying everything here, as perhaps it must with any serious vampire story today, is an AIDS subtext involving sex, infected blood and the plague. Overall, this Dracula could have been less heavy and more deliciously evil than it is, but it does offer a sumptuous engorgement of the senses.

Todd McCarthy.

JACK

July 29–August 4, 1996

Coppola's 'Jack' lacks full-grown drama

A Buena Vista release of a Hollywood Pictures presentation of an American Zoetrope/Great Oaks production. Produced by Ricardo Mestres, Fred Fuchs, Francis Ford Coppola. Executive producer, Doug Claybourne. Directed by Francis Ford Coppola. Screenplay, James DeMonaco, Gary Nadeau. Camera (Foto-Kem color; Technicolor prints), John Toll; editor, Barry Malkin; music, Michael Kamen; production design, Dean Tavoularis; art direction, Angelo Graham; set design, William Beck; set decoration, Armin Ganz, Barbara Munch; costume design, Aggie Guerard Rodgers; sound (Dolby digital), Agamemnon Andrianos; visual effects supervisor, Gary Gutierrez; assistant directors, L. Dean Jones Jr., Gary Scott Marcus; second unit director, Roman Coppola; casting executive, Fred Roos; casting, Linda Phillips Palo, Rosalie Joseph. Reviewed at Walt Disney Studios, Burbank, July 25, 1996. MPAA Rating: PG-13. Running time: 113 mins.

Jack Powell	Robin Williams
Karen Powell	Diane Lane
Miss Marquez	Jennifer Lopez
Brian Powell	Brian Kerwin
Dolores Durante	Fran Drescher
Lawrence Woodruff	Bill Cosby
Paulie	Michael McKean
Bartender	Don Novello
Dr. Benfante	Allan Rich
Louis Durante	Adam Zolotin
Edward	Todd Bosley
John-John	Seth Smith
George	Mario Yedidia
Johnny Duffer	Jeremy Lelliott
Eric	Rickey D'Shon Collins
Victor	Hugo Hernandez

The message of "Jack," as spelled out for all to hear in the climactic scene, is, "None of us have very long on this Earth. Life is fleeting." What, then, is Francis Ford Coppola doing spending a year on this tedious, uneventful fantasy about a boy who ages at four times the normal rate? Surrounded by talent but with very little to do himself, Robin Williams delivers what is probably his first altogether tiresome performance. Disney may be able to promote this into a sizable opening but, as with its hero, longevity is not in the cards.

Something of a companion piece for Coppola to "Peggy Sue Got Married" in the mild, gentle way it deals with a fantastical "what if" situation, new effort has just one thing to say and says it with no sense of surprise or drama. Blandness and lack of daring characterize nearly every minute of the very long two hours, which are marked by a high degree of professionalism at the service of little content.

Initial promise is created by nicely shot costume party and birth scenes, with Karen Powell (Diane Lane), in Wicked Witch getup including red slippers, inexplicably giving birth to a baby boy after just a 10-week pregnancy; through it all, hubby Brian (Brian Kerwin) stands by as a weeping Tin Woodman.

Ten years later, sprig Jack (Williams) is mentally and emotionally his own age but looks 40. Hairy and tall and known to the neighborhood kids as a monster and a freak, Jack has apparently led a cloistered existence all these years in his parents' rambling Victorian house (which looks a lot like the one in "Peggy Sue"). But now that folks have decided to send him to school, Jack and the real world are going to have to come to some understanding.

Naturally, his fifth-grade classmates are mean and unaccepting, at least until Jack proves his worth on the basketball court. Jack cements his standing with the boys when, on a visit to their treehouse,

he brings them a prize copy of Penthouse and shows that he can out-fart them all.

It's never explained whether Jack feels adult-like sexual stirrings, but when the big little man is turned down for a date by his teacher (Jennifer Lopez), he suffers some sort of heart seizure. Shortly thereafter, a butterfly dies on his windowsill, so even he understands that his time may be drawing near.

So what does Jack do? He heads out to a nearby nightclub for a little tea and sympathy from dishy Dolores Durante (Fran Drescher), the very available mother of his best friend. Unfortunately, he lands in a brawl rather than the sack, then goes into a funk over his desire to be just like everyone else.

Using lines they must have overheard at Spago or the Friars Club, screenwriters James DeMonaco and Gary Nadeau have Jack's tutor, played by Bill Cosby, compare his student to a shooting star. Williams then gets to utter the immortal line "I just want to be a regular star," to which Cosby replies, "Jack, you'll never be regular. You're spectacular."

Jack goes back to school in time to hear himself eulogized as "the perfect grown-up," meaning he's adult on the outside but young inside. An epilogue seven years later shows Jack, now a decrepit 68 physically, delivering a valedictory speech at his high school graduation.

In an effective film, this would have been a poignant scene, with Jack's friends moving on to the rest of their lives while he faces the end of his. As it is, the passage is merely sentimental and perfunctory, with the star's old-age makeup all too noticeable.

Pic's highlight by quite a margin is the nightclub scene, sparked by vibrant performances from Drescher and Michael McKean, the latter as a confession-prone stool-sitter who engages Jack in a sex-themed heart-to-heart. Sequence is amusing because it involves Jack's "passing" physically as an adult, which he does effortlessly, while desperately trying to pass in his behaviour as well.

This gives Williams a rare opportunity to stretch emotively, and brings to mind the film that might have been, in which a fully grown 10-year-old, urgently aware of how little time he's got, would desperately try to cram a lifetime of experience into six or seven years. Such a story could have real drama and tragedy as well as high comedy, all elements entirely missing here.

Coppola has brought nothing discernible to the proceedings except his elegant craftsmanship, which does nothing to improve the script. Such contributions as Dean Tavoularis' production design and John Toll's lensing, both enhanced by idyllic Northern California locations, are expectedly first-rate, just as the performers are attractive and professional.

Todd McCarthy.

JOHN GRISHAM'S THE RAINMAKER

November 17, 1997

This 'Rainmaker' pours it on.

A Paramount release of a Constellation Films presentation of a Douglas/Reuther production in association with American Zoetrope. Produced by Michael Douglas, Steven Reuther, Fred Fuchs. Co-producer, Georgia Kacandes.

Directed, written by Francis Ford Coppola, based on the novel by John Grisham. Narration written by Michael Herr. Camera (Deluxe color, Panavision widescreen), John Toll; editor, Barry Malkin; co-editor, Melissa Kent; music, Elmer Bernstein; production design, Howard Cummings; art direction, Robert Shaw, Jeffrey McDonald (San Francisco); set design, Scott Murphy; set decoration, Barbara Murch; costume design, Aggie Guerard Rodgers; sound (Dolby digital), Nelson Stoll; associate producer-assistant director, Gary Scott Marcus; second unit director, Roman Coppola; second unit camera, Bob Yeoman; casting, Linda Phillips-Palo; casting executive, Fred Roos. Reviewed at Paramount Studios, L.A., Nov. 11, 1997. MPAA Rating: PG-13. Running time: 135 mins.

Rudy Baylor	Matt Damon
Kelly Riker	Claire Danes
Leo F. Drummond	Jon Voight
Dot Black	Mary Kay Place
Bruiser Stone	Mickey Rourke
Deck Schifflet	Danny DeVito
Judge Harvey Hale	Dean Stockwell
Miss Birdie	Teresa Wright
Jackie Lemancyzk	Virginia Madsen
Cliff Riker	Andrew Shue
Buddy Black	Red West
Donny Ray Black	Johnny Whitworth
Prince Thomas	Wayne Emmons
Butch	Adrian Roberts

Wilfred Keeley	Roy Scheider
Billy Porter	Randy Travis
Everett Lufkin	Michael Girardin
Jack Underhall	Randall King
F. Franklin Donaldson	Justin Ashforth
B. Bobby Shaw	Michael Keys Hall
Judge Tyrone Kipler	Danny Glover

As carefully constructed, handsomely crafted and flavorsomely acted as a top-of-the-line production from Hollywood's classical studio era, Francis Ford Coppola's screen version of "John Grisham's The Rainmaker" would seem to represent just about all a filmmaker could do with the bestselling author's patented dramatic formulas without subverting them altogether. Although highly predictable in the wake of five previous adaptations of the writer's novels (and the first in which his name is included, Jacqueline Susann- or Sidney Sheldon-style, in the actual title), this story of a young Southern lawyer taking on an evil insurance giant exerts an almost irresistible David and Goliath appeal, and proves absorbing from beginning to end. Paramount release looms as a highly durable B.O. [box office] entry.

Authoring a script on his own for the first time in a very long while, Coppola has adhered to the essential dramatic crescendos important to any Grisham tale, climaxing inevitably in a major courtroom scene in which the little (and young and attractive) guy takes on the establishment or big money or simply long odds. But while not exactly making the material his own, the writer-director has taken his film right up to the edge of undercutting his source without actually doing so, investing it with delightful humor at every possible moment, steering away from the more overt melodramatic elements, and injecting it with a booster shot of cynicism and

unmistakable disenchantment with the legal system.

A quick and tumultuous journey from idealism to jadedness is taken by Rudy Baylor (Matt Damon), a Memphis law school grad who, looking for any experience he can get, goes to work for the aptly named Bruiser Stone (Mickey Rourke), a slimy operator who dresses like a pimp and has never met a scam he didn't like. From Bruiser's shameless leg man Deck Schifflet (Danny DeVito), Rudy learns the basics of ambulance-chasing, which is how he meets Kelly Riker (Claire Danes), who is hospitalized after being beated by her husband with a baseball bat.

Rudy has also generated two potentially promising clients on his own, Miss Birdie (Teresa Wright), an appropriately flighty old woman who may or may not have a large estate to dispose of, and Dot Black (Mary Kay Place), whose son Donny Ray (Johnny Whitworth) is dying of leukemia. The former pans out only to the extent that the penniless Rudy takes up lodgings in back of Birdie's house, while the Blacks seemingly have the making of a real case; the poor family's insurance company, Great Benefit, has flatly rejected all eight attempts made to secure coverage for Donny Ray's care.

Breaking away from Bruiser just as the Feds close in on him, Rudy and Deck, who has never managed to pass the bar exam, set up their own makeshift firm, placing all their bets on the Blacks. At the slightest threat of being taken to court, Great Benefit's slick lawyer Leo F. Drummond (Jon Voight) offers to settle for $75,000.

Playing on the audience's undoubted pleasure in seeing an arrogant and unfeeling corporation being brought down to size, pic methodically presents the clever and lucky ways in which Rudy and Deck peel away the layers of deceit until the venal core of Great Benefit's business practices is laid bare.

Alternate focus lands upon Kelly, a working-class girl whose teenage marriage has turned into a nightmare of beatings and threats. Rudy's own (and a mite convenient) history of abuse at the hands of his father draws him to the almost always bruised and battered young woman.

While Coppola clearly is inspired by the underdog legal team, his ambivalent, philosophical, somewhat jaundiced view of the way of the world restrains him from souping up the picture with manufac- tured frenzy and hysteria, as some Grisham adaptations have done. Pic doesn't go quite so far as saying that all human endeavor is for naught, but its deep sense of disillusion about the legal and business system, conveyed most pointedly in Michael Herr's articulate, sometimes too on-the-nose v.o. [voice- over] narration for Rudy, drifts noticeably in that direction, and concludes the picture on a note of what is best described as upbeat melancholy.

Much of the film's positive mood stems from its unexpected high humor. Coppola has never been particularly known for his comic touch, but here he seems bent on leavening the melodrama with as many laughs as possible, and they are gener- ally honest and well-earned. Much of the amusement comes from DeVito, who tackles his professionally disreputable but personally winning character with his customary relish.

Towering over his cohort, Damon adroitly shades Rudy's transformation from greenhorn to legal eagle, never overdoing his character's sensitivity or momentary triumphs. Voight makes for a super-smooth villain – in the pic's terms, nothing could be worse than someone who represents big law firms *and* the insurance industry. Danes is appealing and capable as the besieged woman, but is hardly tested by the role.

Suppoting cast is rich and deep. Mary Kay Place and Teresa Wright bring to life two quite different isolated women. Mickey Rourke oozes sleaze in his most effective screen appearance in ages, and Dean Stockwell gets a few yocks as an old boys' circuit judge. Most startling and scene-stealing turn comes from Virginia Madsen, who makes the most of her part as a cast-off Great Benefit employee who bravely spills the beans in court about her ex-bosses. Danny Glover goes unbilled in the prominent part of the trial judge.

Production values are immaculate. Memphis locations in autumn create a resplendently somber feel that is echoed in Howard Cummings' production design and John Toll's textured widescreen lens- ing. Barry Malkin's editing moves things along at a determined but not exagger- ated clip, and Elmer Bernstein's score chimes in with some lively and unex- pected sounds.

Todd McCarthy.

Bibliography

Books:

Coppola by Peter Cowie (Andre Deutsch, 1989)
Hollywood's Vietnam by Gilbert Adair (Heinemann, 1989)
Notes: On the Making of Apocalypse Now by Eleanor Coppola
   (Faber & Faber, 1995)
On the Edge: The Life and Times of Francis Coppola by
   Michael Goodwin and Naomi Wise (William Morrow and Co.,
   New York, 1989)
Projections 3 edited by John Boorman and Walter Donohue
   (Faber & Faber, 1994)
Projections 5 edited by John Boorman and Walter Donohue
   (Faber & Faber, 1996)

Articles:

Film Comment Vol. 29 September/October 1993
Films in Review Vol. 42 March/April 1991
Interview Vol. 22 No. 11 November 1992
Premiere Vol. 6 No. 4 December 1992
Premiere Vol. 10 No. 1 September 1996
Premiere Vol. 10 No. 12 August 1997
Starburst No. 175 March 1993
Starburst No. 176 April 1993

Acknowledgements

The author wishes to thank: Robyn Karney, as trusty an editor as she is a friend; his helpful agent Tony Peake; Vito Rocco, who used his sharp film director's eye to pick out many of the splendid photos in this book; Rik Boulton for tracking down rare tapes the author was missing; and Peter Strickland of Sonic Catering for all his valuable assistance.

The publishers would like to thank Photofest, Katz and The Kobal Collection for permission to reproduce the illustrations in this book.

Every reasonable effort has been made to contact the copyright holder of the illustration on page 9 without success. An acknowledgement will be provided in subsequent editions provided notification is sent to the publisher.